Life in War-Torn Bosnia

Titles in The Way People Live series include:

THE WAY
PEOPLE
LIVE

Life in War-Torn Bosnia

by Diane Yancey

Lucent Books, P.O. Box 289011, San Diego, CA 92198-9011

Library of Congress Cataloging-in-Publication Data

Yancey, Diane.
    Life in war-torn Bosnia / by Diane Yancey.
        p.   cm.— (The way people live)
    Includes bibliographical references and index.
    Summary: Examines life in Bosnia before communism, under Tito's rule,
and under present conditions of war.
    ISBN 1-56006-326-2 (alk. paper)
    1. Yugoslav War, 1991- —Bosnia and Hercegovina—Juvenile literature.
2. Bosnia and Hercegovina—History—Juvenile literature.   [1. Yugoslav
War, 1991–   2. Bosnia and Hercegovina—History.]   I. Title.   II. Series.
DR1313.3.Y36   1996
949.7'42—dc20   95-20487
                                                                                          CIP
                                                                                          AC

Printed in the U.S.A.

Contents

Discovering the Humanity in Us All

The Way People Live series focuses on pockets of human culture. Some of these are current cultures, like the Eskimos of the Arctic; others no longer exist, such as the Jewish ghetto in Warsaw during World War II. What many of these cultural pockets share, however, is the fact that they have been viewed before, but not completely understood.

To really understand any culture, it is necessary to strip the mind of the common notions we hold about groups of people. These stereotypes are the archenemies of learning. It does not even matter whether the stereotypes are positive or negative; they are confining and tight. Removing them is a challenge that's not easily met, as anyone who has ever tried it will admit. Ideas that do not fit into the templates we create are unwelcome visitors—ones we would prefer remain quietly in a corner or forgotten room.

The cowboy of the Old West is a good example of such confining roles. The cowboy was courageous, yet soft-spoken. His time (it is always a he, in our template) was spent alternatively saving a rancher's daughter from certain death on a runaway stagecoach, or shooting it out with rustlers. At times, of course, he was likely to get a little crazy in town after a trail drive, but for the most part, he was the epitome of inner strength. It is disconcerting to find out that the cowboy is human, even a bit childish. Can it really be true that cowboys would line up to help the cook on the trail drive grind coffee, just hoping he would give them a little stick of pep-

permint candy that came with the coffee shipment? The idea of tough cowboys vying with one another to help "Coosie" (as they called their cooks) for a bit of candy seems silly and out of place.

So is the vision of Eskimos playing video games and watching MTV, living in prefab housing in the Arctic. It just does not fit with what "Eskimo" means. We are far more comfortable with snow igloos and whale blubber, harpoons and kayaks.

Although the cultures dealt with in Lucent's The Way People Live series are often historically and socially well known, the emphasis is on the personal aspects of life. Groups of people, while unquestionably affected by their politics and their governmental structures, are more than those institutions. How do people in a particular time and place educate their children? What do they eat? And how do they build their houses? What kinds of work do they do? What kinds of games do they enjoy? The answers to these questions bring these cultures to life. People's lives are revealed in the particulars and only by knowing the particulars can we understand these cultures' will to survive and their moments of weakness and greatness.

This is not to say that understanding politics does not help to understand a culture. There is no question that the Warsaw ghetto, for example, was a culture that was brought about by the politics and social ideas of Adolf Hitler and the Third Reich. But the Jews who were crowded together in the ghetto cannot be understood by the Reich's politics. Their life was a day-to-day battle for existence, and the creativity and methods they used to prolong their lives is a vital story of human perseverance that would be denied by focusing only on the institutions of Hitler's Germany. Knowing that children as young as five or six outwitted Nazi guards on a daily basis, that Jewish policemen helped the Germans control the ghetto, that children attended secret schools in the ghetto and even earned diplomas—these are the things that reveal the fabric of life, that can inspire, intrigue, and amaze.

Books in the The Way People Live series allow both the casual reader and the student to see humans as victims, heroes, and onlookers. And although humans act in ways that can fill us with feelings of sorrow and revulsion, it is important to remember that "hero," "predator," and "victim" are dangerous terms. Heaping undue pity or praise on people reduces them to objects, and strips them of their humanity.

Seeing the Jews of Warsaw only as victims is to deny their humanity. Seeing them only as they appear in surviving photos, staring at the camera with infinite sadness, is limiting, both to them and to those who want to understand them. To an object of pity, the only appropriate response becomes "Those poor creatures!" and that reduces both the quality of their struggle and the depth of their despair. No one is served by such two-dimensional views of people and their cultures.

With this in mind, the The Way People Live series strives to flesh out the traditional, two-dimensional views of people in various cultures and historical circumstances. Using a wide variety of primary quotations—the words not only of the politicians and government leaders, but of the real people whose lives are being examined—each book in the series attempts to show an honest and complete picture of a culture removed from our own by time or space.

By examining cultures in this way, the reader will notice not only the glaring differences from his or her own culture, but also will be struck by the similarities. For indeed, people share common needs—warmth, good company, stability, and affirmation from others. Ultimately, seeing how people really live, or have lived can only enrich our understanding of ourselves.

"As You See, Everything Has Changed"

At first the atrocities went almost unnoticed. So many other momentous events were going on in the world—revolution in Russia, bloodshed in the Middle East, famine in Somalia. In the United States, people concentrated on presidential campaigns, economic recession, and the growing AIDS threat.

Yet the evidence was there from the beginning. Observers reported troop movements and war maps that warned of coming violence. "There could be 200,000 to 300,000 people slaughtered within a few months," said one worried official in late 1991.[1]

Then there were the accounts of the war itself. Journalists reported that towns were being shelled, besieged, and burned. Hundreds of thousands of people had been driven from their homes. Neighbor had turned on neighbor. "They are shipping Muslim people through [town] in cattle cars," an anonymous caller told a Western journalist. "Last night there were 25 train wagons for cattle crowded with women, old people and children."[2]

Photographs told their own terrible tale. Starving, half-naked men stared woodenly through barbed wire that encircled the prison camp in which they were held. A woman grimaced in pain as she sprawled in the charred ruins of an open-air market that had just been bombed. A little boy in blue jeans lay dead in a pool of blood, the victim of a sniper.

In Bosnia men, women, and even children are regularly the victims of bombing and sniper attacks. This Bosnian woman cries over the graves of her two sons, both killed while defending Bosnia from the Serbs.

The bloody profile of a civilian woman wounded in the marketplace is testament to the viciousness of the war in Bosnia.

Powder Keg of Europe

The stories and pictures might have come out of Nazi Germany fifty years ago, but they did not. These incidents took place in the 1990s, in the Balkan country of Bosnia-Hercegovina, commonly called Bosnia. Known historically as the "powder keg of Europe," the Balkan countries of Albania, Bulgaria, Greece, and Yugoslavia, located on a peninsula in the southeast corner of Europe, have been notorious for conflict. At times, war stemmed from a desire for freedom as people of the Balkans fought against outsiders who had conquered their land. More often, however, conflicts resulted from ethnic, religious, and cultural differences that had developed within the region over the centuries.

In 1992, these ancient conflicts boiled over when Serbs and Croats—recently part of the same country, Yugoslavia—turned on Bosnian Muslims and each other. The battle-field was Bosnia, a relatively modern, well-ordered republic that had also recently been a part of Yugoslavia. Despite the pinch of a socialist economy, many Bosnians enjoyed the modern comforts of electricity and automobiles. A great number of city dwellers lived in high-rise apartment buildings. Soccer, skiing, and going to movies were popular family pastimes. Tourists who stayed in up-to-date hotels visited Turkish mosques and open-air bazaars, reminders that the Ottoman Empire once ruled the Balkans.

Stunned by Violence

With the coming of the war, all that changed. Serb and Croat attacks on Bosnia's Muslims were both brutal and thorough. An official in the former Republic of Yugoslavia described the effect of the early days of war on Sarajevo, Bosnia's capital city:

And now there is nothing here . . . but an inferno of death, a stench of burning, hunger, tears, men dead and mutilated, mosques, churches and synagogues wrecked, libraries, nursery schools, hotels, museums, residential areas all reduced to heaps of rubble. . . . In short, a city damned, like dozens of other cities . . . ravaged and occupied.[3]

The Bosnian Muslims were unprepared to battle an aggressive and well-armed enemy that seemed bent on their total annihilation. Their lives had been peaceful, even prosperous. The new world was a living nightmare. Children who once played basketball and watched MTV now dodged bullets and watched their friends and families die. Comprehending those changes was almost impossible, as the entry in one young girl's diary reveals. "NINA IS DEAD. A piece of shrapnel lodged in her brain and she died. . . . We went to kindergarten together, and we used to play together in the park. Is it possible I'll never see Nina again?"[4]

As the war continued, world leaders decided to stay out of Bosnia. They deplored the fighting, but treated the conflict as an internal, civil war that would not affect other nations. This attitude by the outside world left Bosnians feeling abandoned and desperate. "Madness is closing in on me little by little," wrote one teen in a letter to a friend.[5] Another young girl from the capital city of Sarajevo admitted, "There's a growing possibility of my killing myself, if all these morons up there and down here [Serb gunmen in the hills and within the town] don't kill me first. . . . I'm human, too, you know, I can only take so much."[6]

Transformed by War

The devastation of Bosnia, unlike the hidden horrors of the Holocaust in the 1940s, has been no secret to the world. An endless

"Will I Ever Go Home Again?"

Naida Zecevic was eighteen years old in 1993. She was one of the many Bosnians forced to flee their country because of the war. Escaping to the United States, Naida wrote of her former life and of her broken dreams in an article entitled "Will I Ever Go Home Again?" published in Newsweek *magazine.*

"We lived in peace for fifty years. We were neighbors, friends—Yugoslavians. I grew up never hearing ethnic hatred or plans for war. I loved summers in Sarajevo, when everyone would walk the long main street in the evening, stopping at cafes filled with friends and happy laughter. My friends and I were normal teenagers. We wanted to have fun, go to movies and parties and shop. We didn't choose friends based on whether we were Serbs, Croats or Muslims. Now I can find no words to express my disappointment in my people or in humanity as a whole. How can I trust friends or neighbors if I return home someday, knowing that they might be willing to kill me?. . .

These are my thoughts as someone living far away from the destruction. Imagine what it's like to actually be there and go through the horror?"

Battered by war, Bosnians continue the daily routine of staying alive, including the constant search for food and water.

stream of pictures and news articles testifies to the brutality practiced against non-Serbs. Letters, carried out of the country with great difficulty, prove that no one has been spared the suffering. As one man writes:

> Let me describe one incident that sums it all up. On exactly the same spot where, not very long ago, policemen clutching walkie-talkies were awaiting the former president of Bosnia-Hercegovina, that same former president and his wife are standing today, bundled up in thick clothes, tending a fire laid between two bricks, preparing their food and coffee and breaking off little branches. As you see, everything has changed.[7]

Scarred by starvation, sickness, torment, and terror, some Bosnians have given in to hate and fear and act with as much brutality as their enemies. Others continue to do what they can to give their lives meaning, whether that is finding food and water or risking death to go to work or to a makeshift school.

What is it like for people whose lives have been turned to rubble by the war? How have they coped with the constant threat of death, with loneliness and separation, with assaults on their traditions, their beliefs, and their humanity? Most importantly, how do the Bosnians continue to hope for a better tomorrow, when new hatreds and resentments threaten to spoil any chance for peace in the future?

A History of Division

Conflict among the people of the Balkans has occurred for centuries. Most citizens of the former Yugoslavia—a country about the size of the state of Wyoming—can trace their ancestry to Slavic tribes whose members migrated from northern Europe in the seventh century. Yet a combination of outside influences helped create enormous differences among the country's various ethnic groups. As Pulitzer Prize–winning journalist Roy Gutman writes, "The history of the people of the Balkans is a tangle of legend and myth, of claims and counterclaims over who did what to whom and when."[8] That tangled history has been marked by clashes as bloody as the war that has ravaged Bosnia in recent times.

A Region Divided

Details about the southern Slavs who occupied the Balkan Peninsula are sketchy. Historians believe they were a warlike people who settled into three loose groups in the region: Slovenes in the north, Croats in the center and west, and Serbs in the southeast. History shows that they often fought among themselves and against outsiders.

Over time the Slavs adapted to cultural differences that had existed in the Balkans since the Roman Empire broke apart in A.D. 395. For instance, Christians in the east spoke Greek and adhered to the Eastern Orthodox Church. Those in the west spoke Latin and practiced their religion in the form of Roman Catholicism. Bosnians, living in the heart of the region, were exposed to both Christian denominations.

The Hungarian Empire gained control of Bosnia for a brief period during the thirteenth century. At about the same time, Serbs to the east were building a rich and independent kingdom under the legendary leadership of King Stephen Dusan. In the early fourteenth century, while Dusan grew more powerful, and Croatia developed an alliance with Hungary, Bosnia regained its independence from the Hungarian Empire. In 1325, under the leadership of Stephen Kotromanic, the country acquired the principality of Hum, later called Hercegovina (or Herzegovina).

Over the next century (1353–1463), civil war and foreign interference continued to plague the Bosnian people. Under the strong leadership of Stephen Tvrtko, however, the country gained considerable influence in the region. Tvrtko was powerful enough to have himself crowned "king of the Serbs, and of Bosnia, and of the Coast," in 1376.[9] For a time, leadership in the Balkans passed from Serbia to Bosnia.

The Turkish Conquest

Maneuvering for control of the region was not over, however. In fact, it had barely begun. Stephen Tvrtko's power proved to be short-lived, as Turks from the Ottoman Empire began to push west into the Balkans. They first defeated a united force of Serbs, Bosnians, Albanians, Croats, Bulgarians, and Hungarians in the Battle of Kosovo in 1389. Then they invaded Bosnia in 1398. By the mid-1400s, Turkish control of Serbia, Bosnia, and parts of Croatia was an accomplished fact.

The coming of the Muslim Turks was a never-to-be-forgotten humiliation for the Serbs. They developed a multitude of myths and songs that celebrated the honor and heroism of the men who died during the Battle of Kosovo. These helped to bolster Serb dignity and their sense of ethnic identity. Serbs hated their Turkish conquerors, and few gave up Orthodox Christianity to embrace the Muslim faith of the Turks.

Bosnians, on the other hand, found many similarities between Islam (the Muslim faith) and Bogomilism, an obscure, heretical form of Christianity they had adopted many years before. Their loyalty to Bogomil beliefs had created almost constant antagonism between themselves and their Roman Catholic and Orthodox neighbors. As historian W. Miller wrote in 1921, many Bosnian Bogomils seemed to find it easy to adopt the Muslim faith. "They had preferred to be conquered by the Sultan than converted by the Pope; and, when once they had been conquered, they did not hesitate to be converted also." [10]

Although Slovenia and Croatia in the north remained under the control of Hungary and Austria, Turkish rule prevailed during the fifteenth and sixteenth centuries in the rest of the Balkan region. Life took on an oriental flavor. Mosques and other Eastern-style buildings dotted the landscape. Children attended Islamic schools. Women shopped in Turkish-style bazaars and prepared Turkish dishes.

The Bogomils

Little is known about the Bogomil religion. Francis R. Jones, an expert on Yugoslavia, gives a thumbnail sketch of the elusive faith in an article entitled "Sleepers Under the Stone," published in the book Why Bosnia?

"Two [Bogomil] texts . . . tell that, in the beginning, God had two sons, Sataniel the elder and Christ [Jesus] the younger. Sataniel, with his angels, rebelled against God. Sataniel, attempting to emulate his father's sublime act of creation, shaped only grotesque parodies: instead of heaven, this earth; instead of the angels, a thing called man. And even then, his creatures would not move or breathe until he had stolen a flame of divine fire and hidden a spark at each man's heart.

Yet this very act was Sataniel's undoing and man's salvation. For God sent Christ, his younger son, to earth—no man he, but pure spirit. . . . And, as fire seeks its source, each spark might turn towards the blaze of light that is the undying Christ. But Sataniel's call is stronger. Few . . . have recognized the light and turned their backs on the two darknesses around them: this earth and this flesh.

But the end is at hand: one day soon Christ will return in glory, destroy utterly all his brother's works, and lead the spirits of the chosen—his father's beloved—into a new Jerusalem."

The Serbs continued to fume under Turkish rule, which grew harsher with the passing of time. A visitor to the region, Lady Mary Wortley Montague, described such conditions in a letter to a friend in 1717:

The inhabitants are industrious, but the oppression of the peasants is so great, they are forced to abandon their houses, and neglect their tillage, all they have being a prey to janissaries [Turkish soldiers], whenever they please to seize upon it.[11]

A National Consciousness

Despite this history of invasion and foreign rule, the southern Slavs managed to retain strong national identities that set them apart both from their conquerors and from each other. Bosnia, for instance, once again fell under the control of Austria-Hungary as Turkish power slipped; yet Bosnians saw themselves as more Oriental than European. Slovenes and Croats resented being treated as second-class citizens under the control of Austria-Hungary, but they considered themselves to be Europeans, nevertheless.

The Serbs, who saw themselves as the traditional leaders in the Balkans, had triumphantly broken free from the Ottoman Empire in 1878. They secretly dreamed of gaining land in Bosnia, where a large number of Serbs lived. This proved impossible in the face of Austrian strength. Independence, however, encouraged Serbs to dream of unity and self-rule for the entire region. Slovenia and Croatia, which were united under French rule for a brief time, also dreamed of creating a single, independent nation for southern Slavs. These dreams sparked hostility toward Austria-Hungary, which kept a tight grip on its holdings in the Balkans.

This hostility reached crisis proportions on June 28, 1914. On that day, the heir to the Austrian throne, Archduke Francis Ferdinand, and his wife, the duchess of Hohenberg, paid a state visit to Sarajevo, the capital of Bosnia. The archduke, long-time supporter of equality for the southern Slavs, hoped that his tour would help ease tensions in the region.

The Powder Keg Sparks War

The royal visit had just the opposite effect. In Sarajevo, thousands of people lined the streets to watch the Austrian couple pass. Some were there protesting the imperialist policies of Austria-Hungary. As the archduke and his entourage proceeded through town en route to a reception, a bomb was thrown at his car. Nedeljo Gabrinovics, a young Bosnian revolutionary, later confessed to the act. The archduke and his wife managed to escape harm, but, upon their return from the reception a few hours later, they were not so fortunate.

Just as they reached the corner of Franz Josef Street, Gavrilo Princip, another Bosnian, sprang out of the crowd and fired several shots at the couple. The archduke and the duchess were rushed to a nearby hospital, but doctors were unable to save their lives.

Since both Gabrinovics and Princip were believed to be ethnic Serbs, Austria-Hungary blamed the assassinations on the Serbian government. "There is no doubt that the attempt on the Archduke was prepared a long time beforehand and that it was excellently organized," declared one Austrian government official.[12] As a result of public demonstrations, martial law was declared in Bosnia to discourage further violence. Days passed, and the tension heightened. Then

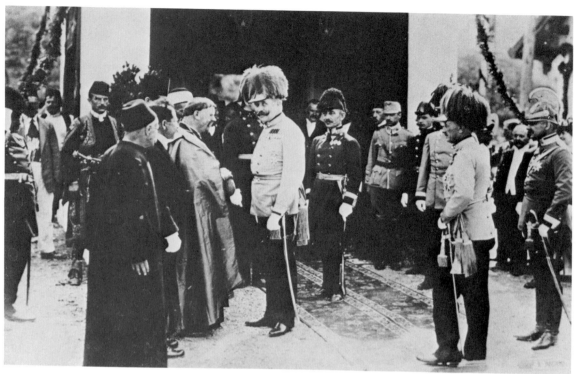

Archduke Ferdinand minutes before his assassination in Sarajevo in 1914. His death sparked World War I.

Austria-Hungary declared war on Serbia on July 28, 1914. In a matter of weeks, the major powers of Europe became involved. World War I had begun.

United or Divided

Although their role in starting World War I was notable, the Balkans did not play a large role in the fighting. The Serb army fought heroically to drive back an Austrian invasion in 1914 and later shared in the final victory over Bulgaria. More important to the Balkan people, however, was the notion of creating an independent country. That vision grew in popularity as time passed. Throughout the war, representatives of the Balkan countries worked together on their dream of national unity for southern Slavs.

With Austria-Hungary's defeat in 1918, that dream became reality. On December 1, 1918, a new country was formed: the Kingdom of the Serbs, Croats, and Slovenes. Participating states were Bosnia and Hercegovina, Croatia, Slovenia, Dalmatia, Montenegro, Serbia, and fragments of land formerly held by Austria and Hungary. The new nation had a democratic, parliamentary government. It officially recognized three national flags and three religions—Roman Catholic, Eastern Orthodox, and Muslim. Peter I of Serbia was named king.

Despite optimism surrounding its creation, the new nation immediately faced a variety of problems. War damage had to be

King Peter faced myriad problems, including ethnic tension, when he ruled the Kingdom of Serbs, Croats, and Slovenes.

Croats, who were jealous of each other's power, debated whether the country should have a centralized government.

Matters finally became so desperate in 1929 that King Alexander, Peter's successor, abolished the constitution and began ruling as dictator. The king was to be "the trustee of the nation until such time as passions had subsided."[13] Alexander changed the name of the country to the Kingdom of Yugoslavia and tried to unite his people by ignoring historical boundaries, reorganizing the government, banning political parties, and restricting the press.

His actions only further angered warring nationalistic groups. In 1934, just as he was considering a return to a constitutional government, the king was assassinated by Croatian terrorists who dreamed of an independent Croatia, free from ties to Yugoslavia. Because Alexander's son, Peter II, was only eleven years old, Prince Paul, the king's cousin, ruled in the boy's place. Prince Paul followed Alexander's policies with little success, and disputes within the country continued.

Hitler's Treachery

The young nation of Yugoslavia faced a bumpy road in the years 1934 to 1940. Weakened by internal conflict, particularly Serb–Croat power struggles, it was unprepared for World War II when it came.

Although strong pro-Western feelings existed among ordinary people, the Yugoslav government had reluctantly signed an agreement with an increasingly aggressive Germany that had already invaded Czechoslovakia, Poland, and France. Officials hoped that an alliance with Adolf Hitler would guarantee Yugoslav sovereignty in case of war.

repaired and debts repaid. Poverty was widespread in rural areas. Industrial development lagged behind Europe except in Croatia and Slovenia in the north. There were only three cities of any size in the whole country: Belgrade, Zagreb, and Subotica. A majority of the Balkan people made their livings as farmers.

In addition to these problems, ethnic groups continued to bicker among themselves. Various attempts to assassinate government officials gave political rivals a chance to hurl accusations back and forth. Elections resulted in uneasy alliances between rival political parties. Serbs and

The people, however, were less optimistic, and in late March Yugoslavs in many cities turned out for anti-German demonstrations.

Hitler retaliated on April 6, 1941, by ordering the German air force to bomb Belgrade, the country's capital. At the same time, German troops and their allies invaded the country. At least ten thousand people were killed and great areas of Belgrade were destroyed. Eleven days after the invasion, the Yugoslav army collapsed. The king and his government fled. Yugoslav citizens were once again occupied by a foreign power that had proved too strong to resist.

World War II was a time of hardship and bloodshed for the people of Yugoslavia. After the invasion, Germany, Italy, Hungary, and Bulgaria assumed control of the country. The

Benevolent Dictator

Although his reign was in fact a dictatorship, King Alexander saw himself as a benevolent despot. In A Short History of Yugoslavia, *edited by Stephen Clissold, historians R. W. Seton-Watson and R. G. D. Laffan describe Alexander's idealistic philosophy.*

"The dictatorship of King Alexander was unlike most of those established in Europe of recent years. It was supported by no organized party and it was announced to be merely a temporary expedient. The king was to be the trustee of the nation until such time as passions had subsided. In the meantime the worst abuses of the parliamentary regime were to be removed. . . . [King Alexander's] proclamation of 6 January said, 'We shall have to seek new methods of work and tread new paths. I am sure that all, Serbs, Croats and Slovenes, will loyally support my efforts, whose sole aim will be to establish as rapidly as possible such administration and organization of the state as will best conform with the general needs of the people and the interests of the state.'"

Eager to establish order in the young nation of Yugoslavia, King Alexander established himself as a "benevolent dictator."

conquerors were not tolerant of the people they defeated. Jews and Serbs were slaughtered in areas occupied by Hungary. Germany was merciless to those it controlled, as well. A Yugoslav citizen remembered one frightening incident:

> Fifty-two people who were in the streets, who only *happened* to be out in the streets when the Germans and the Hungarians came to our town on that morning in 1941. The soldiers shot them. On sight, without a word. All of them.[14]

One of Germany's first actions was to establish a puppet government in Croatia, one of Yugoslavia's northern states. Under German command, the soon-to-be notorious Ustasi—Croatian troops who collaborated with Italian and German forces—then began killing Serbs, Jews, and Gypsies in both Croatia and Bosnia. At times, the acts of violence were so heinous that even Germans—themselves guilty of killing millions of Jews, Gypsies, and other minorities—were shocked. Serbs were quick to recognize the killings for what they were—a Croatian desire to rid

Beset by troubles, Yugoslavia was no match for Hitler's aggressive German army (pictured).

German troops capture a group of Yugoslav resistance fighters during World War II.

their state of non-Croats, and to wipe out neighbors who might possibly pose a threat in the future.

As the occupation of Yugoslavia continued, rebellious Yugoslavs began to develop secret resistance movements in order to fight against their enemies. Armed groups of Serbs, known as Chetniks, organized in Serbia. The best-known Chetniks were followers of Colonel Draza Mihajlovic, a Serb nationalist and strong anti-Communist. Because Mihajlovic supported the Allies (Britain, France, the United States, and the Soviet Union), he and his troops were at first recognized by the Allies as the principal leaders of Yugoslav resistance.

Another resistance group, the Partisans, soon gained world attention, however. Their leader was a Croatian-Slovenian peasant named Josip Broz Tito. Tito was a Communist who had taken part in the Bolshevik (Communist) Revolution in Russia. Upon his return to Yugoslavia, he allied himself with the Partisans. Their war slogan ("Death to Fascism, Freedom to the People") won them recruits across the country.

Tito and his Partisans, the nucleus of which were Communists, worked valiantly to fight Nazi invaders and Ustasi forces during the war. At times, the resistance fighters faced such adversity that going on seemed impossible. Tito described some of the conditions they endured in a message for help, sent to Georgi Dimitrov, a fellow Communist:

Hundreds of thousands of refugees are threatened by death from starvation. Is it really impossible after twenty months of heroic, almost superhuman fighting to find some way to help us? . . . Typhus has now started to spread and we are without drugs. People are dying like flies from starvation.[15]

Grisly Trophies

In her biography, Tito, *author Phyllis Auty describes World War II atrocities, which contributed to the hatred that consumes the people of the former Yugoslavia today.*

"Partisans and civilian populations, especially in country districts in Bosnia and Croatia, suffered terrible losses. There were many deaths from starvation and endemic typhus as well as from enemy operations. Thousands of Yugoslavs also died as a result of . . . the fighting between Partisans and Cetniks [Chetniks]. . . . [In] south Serbia, Cetniks slaughtered Muslims to try to create a homogeneous Serbian population in regions they claimed as their Serbian homeland. In Bosnia and Croatia great numbers of Orthodox Serbs were killed on account of their religion. . . . In Croatia massacres of many thousands of Serbian men, women and children were carried out by special Ustasi bands with atrocities so bestial as to be incredible were they not attested beyond dispute. A frequently repeated story was of Ustasi who collected eyes or other parts of their victims' bodies and boasted of the tally. A British doctor wrote that he himself saw such grisly trophies. 'Stepping forward I took the bag lying on the table and opened it. At first I thought it was a bag of shelled oysters, then on looking closer, I saw they were human eyes.'"

Despite hunger and illness, the Partisans continued to fight. They were working toward greater ends than simply winning the war. They hoped to discredit Mihajlovic's Chetnik forces and gain power and prestige in the eyes of the world. They dreamed of being in control of Yugoslavia when the war ended.

By 1943, Allied leaders were convinced that the Partisans were the most effective resistance group fighting the Germans in Yugoslavia. They gave Tito their support. With the help of the Allies, the Partisans succeeded in defeating the Germans and driving Ustasi and Chetnik forces into hiding. And, by the end of the war, Tito and his Communist colleagues had accomplished another goal. They had emerged as sole rulers of Yugoslavia.

A New Era

As head of the Communists, Tito believed that he could unite his country and control the hostility that had existed for centuries among the people of the Balkans. For forty years, through a combination of ingenuity, charisma, and ruthlessness, he managed to achieve his goal. Yugoslavia became "a bright spot amid the general grayness of Eastern Europe."[16]

Despite Tito's skill, however, Yugoslavs did not forget their bloody history. Ethnic tensions remained unresolved. Those tensions would bubble to the surface again just when the world had come to hope that the powder keg of Europe had been permanently defused.

CHAPTER 2

Tito and the Good Life

The end of World War II found the people of Yugoslavia living in chaos and destitution. For five years, the country had been divided and occupied by enemy powers. The war had claimed more than 1.5 million Yugoslav lives, over 10 percent of the prewar population. About a million of those people had been killed by other Yugoslavs. The country's major cities, industries, and communication systems had been destroyed. Great numbers of men, women, and children faced starvation.

"An Outstanding Personality"

Into the chaos stepped Josip Tito, war hero and victorious leader. Tito was an imposing man, as Sir John Slessor, Air Force Chief of Staff for Allied forces in the Middle East, described.

I was immediately impressed with him and have since had good reason to return to the opinion I then formed of him, that

Historian Rebecca West visited the Balkans in 1939, a decade before Tito came to power and began modernizing his nation. West recorded her reactions to the backwardness of the region in her book, Black Lamb and Grey Falcon.

"On our way again, . . . poverty was all about us. The mosques were no longer built of stone and bricks, but were roughly plastered like farm buildings, with tiled roofs and rickety wooden minarets. But they had still a trace of elegance in their design; and there were fine embroideries on the boleros the women wore over their white linen blouses and dark full trousers, and on the shirts of the black-browed men. With some of these people we could not get on friendly terms. If they were in charge of horses they looked at us with hatred, because the horses invariably began to bolt at the sight of the automobile, however much we slowed down. We sent two hay-carts flying into the ditch. So rarely had these people seen automobiles that they looked at us with dignified rebuke. . . . But the people who had no horses to manage looked at us with peculiar respect, since automobiles passed so rarely."

he was much more than a guerrilla leader—an outstanding personality and potentially a statesman of no mean order. . . . A fine looking man, he was also very intelligent.[17]

Tito's Communist forces already controlled the army and many local governments. Now they got to work setting a new political and economic direction for their country. Led by Tito, a new Yugoslav parliament met on November 29, 1945. One of its first actions was to abolish the monarchy—the kings had too often identified themselves with Serb rather than Yugoslav interests. The new parliament declared Yugoslavia a democratic nation made up of six republics—Bosnia-Hercegovina, Croatia, Slovenia, Serbia, Montenegro, and Macedonia—and two provinces: Kosovo and Vojvodina. The new nation was called the Federal People's Republic of Yugoslavia, later renamed the Socialist Federal Republic of Yugoslavia.

Titoism

Yugoslavs soon discovered that despite its claim to be a democracy, their new nation was a dictatorship, complete with government controls and secret police. Wartime collaborators and so-called enemies of the state were rounded up and executed. Political criticism was quashed; religious practices were discouraged.

Tito led the Communist Party, the government, and the armed forces. He also set up a Soviet-style, socialist economic system, under which the government seized most private land and encouraged people to work on large state-owned cooperative farms. Wages were set by the government, which established a five-year plan that emphasized the development of heavy industry.

All this infuriated ordinary Yugoslavs. They resented being forced to give up land their families had owned for centuries. They did not want to work for low pay and little responsibility. "They became tired of over-work, dirt and discomfort," wrote historian Phyllis Auty. "From foreigners who came into the country they saw that others who had not suffered so much during the war had better clothes, food, [medicine], more luxuries and an easier life."[18] In the 1950s, a farmworkers' revolt coupled with a drought caused agricultural production to drop sharply. Soon the nation was again threatened with starvation.

But Tito had already begun to take daring steps that he believed would make his people happier. "Life had taught me that the most dangerous thing at such critical moments is not to take a stand. . . . In such situations, reactions must always be bold and determined."[19]

His plan was quite simple. He abandoned strict Communist policies and turned to the United States and western Europe for economic help. It was an unheard-of move for a conventional and obedient Communist, but it accomplished its purpose. Conditions began to change for the better.

Then Tito introduced another bold economic reform. As *The New York Times* described:

Tito and the Communists were in full control of Yugoslavia after the war. This photo from the 1940s shows Yugoslav children giving the Communist salute.

What emerged in Yugoslavia was to become known as Titoism, a brand of Communism with free-market forces, consumerism, Western publications at the newsstands, . . . a decision-sharing role for employees called workers' self management, and, importantly, freedom for virtually all citizens to travel abroad and to return at will.[20]

As a result, most collective and state farms were dissolved. Farmers were again allowed to work their own land, and to decide what they would grow and how much they would produce. Enthusiastic entrepreneurs created a multitude of small businesses such as beauty parlors, repair shops, restaurants, and grocery stores. Even big business profited from the change. The country began to grow and modernize. Between 1957 and 1960, Yugoslavia showed the second highest economic growth rate in the world.

For Their Health

Ensuring the economic well-being of his country was only a first step. Tito realized that the good life would be no more than a dream if Yugoslavs were crippled by illness and disease, so he set about improving the physical health of the citizens.

Most ordinary Yugoslavs had never been taught good health practices. No one knew that food must be stored safely and that drinking water should be pure. No one understood that children should be vaccinated against disease. In times of illness or injury, most people relied on folk remedies and each other for help. Thus, serious disease was rampant. Every year, thousands of people needlessly suffered and died from tuberculosis, diphtheria, dysentery, and whooping cough. Often

there was only one doctor and no hospital in a region of several thousand people.

Hospitals themselves were scarce, unsanitary, and understaffed places where people got sicker almost as often as they got well. Journalist Priscilla M. Harding wrote about conditions during a typhus epidemic in 1914:

> In March the typhus death rate was fifty daily and there were over a thousand cases in Belgrade. . . . Soon the disease spread among the [hospital] personnel, whose number had already been reduced by five. . . . This left only nine nurses and one surgeon in the big hospital.[21]

Tito's government set about improving those conditions dramatically. Epidemic diseases were brought under control as more physicians and nurses were trained, hospitals and medical facilities were built and modernized, and people were educated regarding good health practices. Thanks to the government, most Yugoslavs were soon covered by health insurance that made going to the doctor more practical.

Life was also cushioned by a welfare system that provided support for the poor, elderly, and mentally or physically handicapped. Because family was judged to be important to all Yugoslavs even though many women worked, the government paid new mothers to take generous maternity leave. Working mothers also received paid leave to care for sick children.

Men, Then Women

While vital to the family, women had traditionally taken second place to men in prewar Yugoslav society. They expected little from life beyond marriage, raising children, and

Tito did not adhere to strict Communist doctrine, and living conditions in postwar Yugoslavia improved dramatically.

managing the home. Author Rebecca West, who visited the country just before World War II, noted the slavelike conditions under which men kept their wives in her book *Black Lamb and Grey Falcon:*

> Their women have to wait on them while they eat, must take sound beatings every now and again, work till they drop, even while child-bearing, and walk while their master rides.[22]

With the war, much of that changed. Enormous numbers of men were killed, and women had to take over family responsibilities. Tito's postwar government encouraged women to continue to make such changes, even going so far as to print a variety of magazines—*Women's World*, *Today*, and *Woman*, for example—in which women's rights were explained and defended. Tito himself disapproved of the way men treated their wives.

> It not infrequently happens that even party members have an uncomradely attitude towards their wives, and even beat them. Others are still inclined to marry several times. . . . All this greatly impairs the prestige, both of the comrades themselves, and of the party.[23]

Yugoslav women at work in a watch factory. Under Tito, Yugoslav women gained greater rights and were free to work, go to school, and engage in politics.

As time passed, Yugoslavia's male-dominated society moderated somewhat. Women were granted complete civil and political rights. Many still remained at home, but others went out to work, went to college, and got involved in politics.

Those in the workplace faced obstacles similar to those of women throughout the world. They were paid less than their male coworkers. Often they could not reach top administrative levels in business and were channeled into three general career fields: social welfare, public services, and trade and catering. For instance, almost all Yugoslavia's elementary school teachers were female. Still, like women everywhere, they remained determined and hopeful. "It will be different for my daughters," predicted Milena Radic, who had married young and never left her husband's country village. "With an education, I'm sure [they] will have a better life."[24]

Study, Study

In postwar Yugoslavia, many people came to recognize education as the key to a better future. Before World War II, they had all but ignored schooling; only slightly more than one-quarter of all children enrolled in primary school, which involved just four years of formal training. Children in rural areas—and Yugoslavia was predominantly rural—often did not go to school at all.

In his efforts to modernize his country, Tito placed strong emphasis on education. He rebuilt school buildings and libraries, established new schools, and retrained teachers. Children were sent to school for eight years of primary education, and their schedules bulged with required subjects. Author Lila Perl described the program of one young Yugoslav, Marija Maksimovic:

> Yugoslav children usually take up the study of either Russian or English in grade school, as their first foreign language. Marija takes Russian and finds it difficult. . . . In addition to Russian, Marija is studying mathematics, European history, geography, biology, technical drawing, music, physical education, art, home economics and Serbian language— eleven subjects in all.[25]

With the new emphasis on education, enrollment in secondary schools rose dramatically, and students were encouraged to get a university education if possible, although tuition was high. Between 1939 and 1987, the number of university students increased from twenty thousand to over three hundred thousand.

Ironically, as students got together and exchanged ideas, they often became highly critical of the Communist government that had promoted their education and awareness. They were quick to point out injustices and to demand change, despite the government's efforts to suppress their complaints.

Nature of the People

If Tito's efforts to promote education were successful, his attempts to eliminate worship were not. Unlike education, religion had always played a large part in the lives of Yugoslavs, and it continued to do so. Few towns or villages existed that did not boast at least three houses of worship: a mosque, an Orthodox church, and a Roman Catholic church.

For a time, the Communist government strongly discouraged all religious practices, took over church land, and frowned on formal religious instruction. Immediately after the war, many members of the clergy were oppressed, even killed. Because some Catholic clergy had condoned many wartime atrocities—particularly the persecution of Serbs—numerous priests were executed or imprisoned.

Later, however, Tito became more tolerant and relaxed restrictions somewhat. People who went to religious services might be penalized with low-paying, low-status jobs, but little more. One young Yugoslav explained the theory she believed lay behind the more relaxed policy:

> Our President Tito—and I mean this sincerely—is much too wise [to prohibit anyone from going to church]. He knows the nature of the Yugoslav people. If you tell them they may not do such-and-such they will insist on doing it. But if you say they *may* do something, they will usually not bother. . . . The older ones still go to

church; many of the younger ones like myself don't care to.[26]

Though many of the younger generation were brought up to believe religion was unimportant, Yugoslavs for the most part observed their religious traditions, which were also tied to much of their culture and history. Serbs were loyal to the Eastern Orthodox Church, Croats to Roman Catholicism, Muslims to their Islamic heritage.

Those religious loyalties, which came complete with ethnic hostilities and prejudices, proved to be an indelible part of Yugoslav memory. Tito and the Communists had smothered their expression; still, they would play an important role in the breakup of the country after Tito died and the Communists were no longer in control.

"Leaping the Centuries"

As change swept the country, Yugoslavia became a curious combination of the old and the new, a nation whose people clung to their traditions while trying to adapt to the exciting new world their leaders were creating for them.

A large part of that new world was found in cities. As Yugoslavia rebuilt and industrialized, thousands of people—particularly young people—left family farms to find work and a better life in urban centers that were

As change swept Yugoslavia under Tito's rule, huge numbers of citizens migrated to cities.

growing up across the country. By 1985, the number of people working in urban industry had grown from a little over one million to over six million.

So rapid was the change from rural to urban that some families had trouble keeping up with it. One Yugoslav described a peasant household whose members inappropriately carried their livestock with them when they moved to town.

> There they were, living comfortably on the sixteenth floor of a modern elevator apartment building, eating eggs from their chickens and drinking goat's milk just as they always had done in their primitive cottage. . . . You see how difficult it is for our people to keep up with the times. We are moving very fast, leaping the centuries, here in Yugoslavia.[27]

The flow of people to cities resulted in serious housing shortages that plagued Yugoslavia for generations. Single men often made do by living in stark dormitory-style buildings provided by the businesses for which they worked. Government workers were supposedly guaranteed space in one of the country's newly built apartment houses, but units often were unavailable to those without money or connections in the Communist Party. Families might live for years crowded into homes with numerous relatives while waiting for a government-owned apartment to become empty. Bitter disputes often arose among candidate families when an opening did occur.

Building a home of one's own was a popular option, but it, too, had drawbacks. Cost was the first and foremost problem. Shortages of building materials coupled with bureaucratic red tape made building a house extremely expensive. Couples often invested up to twenty times their annual income when buying property and building materials. Even then, the new home might be less than perfect. Construction usually took place on the edge of town, and poorly planned developments sometimes lacked paved streets, running water, and sewer lines.

A Comfortable Life

Over time, however, people adjusted to such complications. The Communist economy was restrictive, but in many respects, life was similar to life in many other cities around the world. People got married and had children. Men went to the office in the morning carrying a briefcase and wearing a business suit and tie. Women worked, too, and in their free time shopped in supermarkets and department stores, using credit for more expensive purchases. If both husband and wife were employed, the couple often placed their young children in a government-run care center for the day.

The workday ended for many Yugoslavs between two and three o'clock, leaving them free to eat dinner at home, visit friends, and be with family. Home life was comfortable and relaxed. "We children . . . are wondering whether to take a walk, play a game, watch a movie on TV or play the unavoidable Scrabble," wrote one young girl.[28] Watching television, talking on the telephone, and listening to rock music were popular teen pastimes.

As in other countries, holidays such as Christmas were occasions for family gatherings. Birthdays meant a special meal, with cake and presents. Other entertainment included dining out at a restaurant, going to the theater, a museum, or a park, or taking a vacation in another country. France and Italy were favorite destinations of many Yugoslavs.

A butcher shop bustles with activity as shoppers choose from an abundant inventory. Although the Communist economy was restrictive, people in Yugoslavia led fairly comfortable, secure lives.

In the Country

Despite the attraction of life in the city, many Yugoslavs remained in the country, where conditions gradually improved as well. Some people chose to live on their farms and commute to nearby towns to work. With the extra earnings, they were able to enlarge their homes, purchase farm machinery, and splurge on vacations to the mountains or the ocean. Many homes had electricity. Proud homemakers purchased refrigerators, washing machines, and other modern conveniences, although these were expensive and sometimes hard to get.

Yet even with improvements, rural life was relatively simple. Some homes were large and elegant, but most were boxlike with red tile roofs. Typically, country dwellers grew lush vegetable gardens in the backyard and cured their meat in a smokehouse by the back door. Regular pastimes revolved around trips to the village marketplace, church, or mosque. Friends and family spent evenings together chatting over beer or coffee in local *kafanas* (coffeehouses).

The Importance of Family

Whether in cities or in the countryside, family played a central role in Yugoslav society. A family group—traditionally called the *zadruga*—was typically large, made up of parents, children, grandchildren, cousins, and second cousins, all of whom might live in the same house under the authority of the oldest male family member. So important were families in Yugoslavia that under Tito, laws were passed to ensure that responsibilities were not neglected. For instance, one piece of legislation required family members to support their needy or elderly relatives.

Yugoslavs knew that there were great advantages to being part of a large, close-knit family, especially in the country. When land was owned in common, everyone shared the burden of work, especially during harvest and planting seasons. When husband and wife held jobs in nearby towns, female relatives ran the household and looked after small children, while male family members other than the wage earner took responsibility for working the family land.

As time passed and modern conveniences let couples become more self-reliant, the extended family lost some of its impor-

tance. More and more often, a couple and their children were the sole residents in a house or apartment, although relatives might live nearby. In the extended families that remained, older family members often had trouble retaining their traditional authority in the face of changing times and practices.

"Young people are different nowadays," complained Milan Radic, an older Yugoslav who shared a home with three generations of family. "They want to go to the cities and live in tall buildings with modern conveniences. They don't care for the old ways any longer."[29]

Despite the changes, family ties remained important to most Yugoslavs. Students or single family members who moved to the city to work or study often depended on relatives to house them. Migrants to the city turned to the family back home for support and encouragement.

By the 1970s, under Tito's firm control, life for most Yugoslavs had improved dramat-

The Zadruga

The zadruga developed in early Slav times because people needed to bond together for protection against enemies. This excerpt from Phyllis Auty's biography, Tito, *describes the ancient institution.*

"In a *zadruga* all related members of a family lived together in one house or group of buildings under the authority of its head, usually the oldest male. . . . *Zadrugas* varied in size from two or three married couples with their children to as many as a hundred families living together. The principle was that sons stayed in the *zadruga*, bringing home their brides and building on extra

sleeping huts till the whole *zadruga* looked like a beehive. Daughters joined their husband's *zadruga* as they married. Under the *Gospodar* [head male] every member had a place in a social hierarchy in which age had priority, but any males were superior to females. The *Gospodar* had patriarchal authority over all members, and his wife ordered the life and work of the women, who prepared communal meals which were eaten together. Major decisions about communal property, work on the land and other matters were taken after consultation between the males."

Never Had It So Good

In his article "The Promise of Self-Management," published in the Progressive *magazine, journalist Sidney Lens describes the life of a typical Yugoslav in 1981. As Lens points out, life under Tito was both comfortable and secure.*

"My friend Juliana . . . now shares a modern three-room apartment with her retired mother; they used to share a flat [apartment] with another family. She has a color television set made in Japan, which she bought on the installment plan. She earns $290 a month, which together with her mother's $100 monthly pension provides them with a modest income. But Juliana's rent is only $18 a month, medical care is free, and she can retire at age fifty-five and draw 85 per cent of her present earnings for the rest of her life—plus a cost-of-living adjustment that guarantees the pension's purchasing power.

Though she complains constantly that she is strapped for funds, Juliana travels out of the country several times a year—usually to Austria, but also to London and Paris. She could work in Frankfurt [Germany], and earn higher wages, particularly since she is fluent in German, but the thought has never occurred to her. Instead, she remains in Belgrade, complains—as almost everyone does—about constantly rising prices, but admits she has never had it so good. 'My mother,' she adds, 'told me the same thing last week—that in all her years she has never lived so well.'"

ically. They were respected worldwide as a nation, united as a country, and able to enjoy many of the good things of life. Their venerable leader, who had piloted them through bad times and good, was acclaimed by many as a hero, "the first and only Yugoslav."[30]

The peace and prosperity that Yugoslavs enjoyed, however, was destined to end when Tito died. The veteran dictator had recognized the potential for power struggles in the government after his passing. Therefore, "with the aim of averting rivalries and concentrations of power," he had established a rotating eight-member State Presidency, with one member chosen from each of the country's six republics and two provinces.[31] After Tito's death in 1980, each of the eight would take its turn as one-year head of the federal government. Each republic and province also had a president, who held considerable power in his own region.

Tito, however, had not foreseen the widespread changes that would occur in the world after his death. In the 1980s, Communist countries such as the Soviet Union, Poland, and East Germany faced serious economic problems. In Yugoslavia, food shortages, labor strikes, and financial scandals threatened the country's stability. Prices skyrocketed. Workers lost their jobs. Tension grew between republics that blamed each other for the hard times.

The collective State Presidency lacked the insight and skill it needed to steer the country through the rocky years. Unrest in Yugoslavia grew. Out of that unrest developed the most savage and divisive war of modern times.

Fury of War

By the late 1980s, the image of Yugoslavia as a nation of strong, independent people peacefully coexisting under the banner of Communism had faded. The power of the Communists collapsed in 1990, opening the door for a variety of political parties, free elections, and new leadership. Citizens in most republics were eager to embrace democracy, with all the freedom and responsibility that went along with it.

Serb Strongman

In the Republic of Serbia, however, citizens voted to retain the Socialist (formerly Communist) government with which they were familiar. This decision was due, in part, to Slobodan Milosevic, a Communist turned nationalist who became president of Serbia in 1989.

Milosevic was known for his ruthlessness and love of power. One European diplomat described him as "a brigand and a fanatic, but a sly, intelligent and sophisticated one." During Milosevic's rise to the presidency, he had gained control of the Republic of Serbia through censorship of newspapers and books. He "turned television into an instrument of personal power," by allowing only programs that supported his political views to be aired.[32] He used federal troops to forcibly bring an end to self-rule in the independent provinces of Kosovo and Vojvodina, thus making them unwilling extensions of Serbia.

Not only did Milosevic believe in holding strict control over his republic, he also felt that Yugoslavia's six republics should remain together as one country. His expressed intention was to gain control of all parts of Yugoslavia populated by Serbs—to create a "Greater Serbia." His unstated purpose was to grab as much land and power as possible. To do that he needed the support of at least a portion of his people.

Jurij Bajec, a former colleague, understood Milosevic's talent for rallying support for his radical ideas. "He knew how to touch the Serbs' national feelings. That became his main winning card, and he knew it would make millions come to hear him speak."[33]

"It's Serbia That's Under Attack"

Serbs were the most numerous of the ethnic groups in Yugoslavia—over one-third of the population. They took great pride in their heritage and the heroic deeds of their forefathers. President Milosevic encouraged that pride. He also stirred up Serb grievances against their neighbors by reminding them of the tyranny they had suffered in the past. For instance, government-sponsored brochures were illustrated with old photographs of severed Serb heads and referred to Croat atrocities during World War II. The news reported imaginary threats of violence by Croats and Muslims against the people of Serbia.

Slobodan Milosevic fueled ethnic unrest in Yugoslavia after he became president of Serbia in 1989.

Government-controlled television and radio repeatedly hinted that Bosnian Muslims were "fundamentalists" who wanted to drive out Serbs and set up an Islamic Republic in the heart of the Balkans. One Serb explained:

> [All] Muslims are in this together. They have big families in order to swamp Serbia and Yugoslavia with Muslims, and turn Yugoslavia into a Muslim republic. . . . They will continue to advance until they have taken Vienna, Berlin, Paris, London—all the great cities of Europe. Unless they are stopped.[34]

The government was not the only source of propaganda against non-Serbs. In schools, children studied such works as the epic poem "The Mountain Wreath," which glorifies the destruction of the Islamic culture and urges the slaughter of Muslims. In many bookstores, Serbs could buy the novels and essays of Dobrica Cosic, who portrays Serbs as a superior people who were often victims of ethnic persecution. As one Serb journalist explained in 1993, "The average Serb honestly believes it's Serbia that's under attack."[35]

Neighboring republics worried about Milosevic and his talk of Serb superiority and a Greater Serbia. Most Serbs lived in their own republic, but some were scattered throughout Yugoslavia, particularly Croatia and Bosnia-Hercegovina. Would those Serb exiles remain loyal to the republics in which they lived? Or might they align with Milosevic?

Moves for Independence

Partly as a result of this worry, partly because of a desire for self-rule, many citizens of other republics decided that their best interests lay in a move to become more independent of Milosevic and the Serb-led federal government. In the spring of 1990, Croatia and Slovenia held their first free elections. Citizens in both republics voted for multiparty, Western-oriented governments. New provisions in their constitutions affirmed the people's right to secede from Yugoslavia if their "national self-determination" was not guaranteed.

In the fall of 1990, the republics of Macedonia and Bosnia-Hercegovina followed in Slovenia and Croatia's footsteps. The Bosnian people elected a multiparty government that accurately reflected the ethnic mix of the overall population: 99 Muslims, 83 Serbs, 50 Croats. Muslim Alija Izetbegovic became the first non-Communist leader of the republic.

The Serb government, led by Milosevic, announced that a breakup could take place only if boundaries were redrawn to make all Serb-inhabited land part of Serbia. This was not likely to happen; Croats and Muslims also lived in those regions, and any boundary change meant that Croatia and Bosnia would have to give up portions of their territory. If they did not, however, Milosevic vowed to go to war to keep Yugoslavia together.

Events came to a head in May 1991. At that time, Stipe Mesic, a Croat, was scheduled to take his seat as head of the revolving State Presidency that had been set up by Tito shortly before his death. The Serbs blocked this move, and, on June 25, Croatia and Slovenia declared their formal independence from Yugoslavia. In the coming year, presidents and parliament members of all but two of the republics seceded from the federal government. All that remained of the former country of Yugoslavia were Serbia and Montenegro.

Nowhere to Run

Concerned about reported humanitarian abuses in Croatia and Bosnia, delegates from Catholic churches in the United States visited the former Yugoslavia in 1992. The group was told by officials that there were no refugees at the Bosnian-Croatian border. What the delegates saw, however, was related by an archbishop, Theodore McCarrick of Newark, New Jersey, and published in America magazine.

"We saw thousands and thousands of these people trying to get across—men who had sent their wives and children on ahead of them while they tried to defend their property with shotguns and hunting rifles and pistols against the fifth largest army of the world, the Yugoslav Army.

They surrounded our group, and for a moment a couple of us felt, 'Somebody will get the idea of taking us hostage and negotiating safe passage across.' So I spoke up and said, 'I wanted to come see you because I was told you were not here'—someone was translating for me —'and I promise when I go back we will tell the world about you.' That changed the whole thing, and they said: 'Go, go quickly and tell the world.'

You know, you don't always have the chance to look into people's faces and see that terrible fear that, 20 kilometers away, there is a juggernaut [a terrible force] that will not just take them prisoners but that will wipe them out. You can actually see in those faces what a terrible thing it is to be a refugee."

"This Is Hell"

One day after Croatians and Slovenians declared their independence, the federal Yugoslav People's Army (YPA) rolled across their borders.

Dominated by Serbs, the YPA had naturally aligned itself with Milosevic and his followers as Yugoslavia began to split apart. The YPA was one of the largest military forces in Europe, although not comparable in size or scope to U.S. military forces. Troops numbered over 150,000 active-duty soldiers, sailors, and air personnel, in addition to hundreds of thousands of trained reservists. The Yugoslav air force operated hundreds of combat aircraft and armed helicopters; its navy boasted vessels such as submarines, minesweepers, missile boats, and amphibious landing craft. Heavy artillery included rocket launchers, surface-to-air missiles, and antitank guns.

Despite the forces at his command, Milosevic soon realized that Slovenians were too well armed and well organized to be easily defeated. In addition, he saw that he had little to gain by blocking Slovenia's move for independence because few Serbs lived in that republic. Thus he allowed Slovenia to break away with little fuss or bother.

Croatia, however, was a different story. Croatian Serbs, who made up nearly 12 percent of the population, reacted strongly against that republic's declaration of independence. Defiantly, they formed autonomous zones within Croatia and attacked their Croat neighbors. Milosevic promptly declared Serb lives to be in danger and sent federal troops into the new republic. Officially, they were a peacekeeping force, but they soon abandoned their position of neutrality and actively fought on the side of the Serbs.

By the summer of 1991, an all-out war was in progress in Croatia. Serb planes and heavy artillery hammered the town of Vukovar on the Danube River. Serb gunboats positioned themselves off the Croatian coast and shelled the walled city of Dubrovnik, targeting centuries-old monuments. Hundreds of homes, churches, and businesses were destroyed. Families crouched in cellars for days without food and water. The stench of decaying corpses—livestock, pets, and human bodies—filled the air.

"This is hell," declared one television reporter. "We just cannot stand it anymore."[36]

In response to the attacks, the United Nations (UN) quickly declared an arms embargo to cut off the flow of additional weapons into the former Yugoslavia. At the same time, UN peacekeeping troops were sent into the area. An uneasy peace was eventually established, but by then, Serb forces occupied almost one-third of Croatia.

Croatian Dreams

Although the central motivation for Milosevic's attacks against Croatia was a drive for land and power, Serb fear of Croat aggression was not entirely unjustified. Many Croats, Yugoslavia's second largest ethnic group, had strong nationalistic feelings and long-held dreams of carving a "Greater Croatia" out of land in Serbia and Bosnia. Like the Serbs, many Croats had settled in these neighboring republics over time, and they viewed the land they occupied as their own.

The new president of Croatia, Franjo Tudjman, was an ardent nationalist as well. He put Croatia's interests above all others. When it suited him politically, Tudjman collaborated with Serbs; at other times he was Bosnia's friend. Tudjman vowed to "fight and defend our homeland," against Serb invasion.[37] At the same time he appeared ready to invade his neighbors if that meant gaining land for Croatia.

"The Atmosphere Was Being Prepared"

Multicultural Bosnia, sitting in the center of the Balkans, was caught in the middle of tensions and ambitions that motivated its neighbors. Serbia lay to the east, Croatia to the north and west. On their way to make war with Croatia, Serb troops had boldly marched through Bosnia. A few months later, federal troops were stationing themselves inside Bosnia's borders. Milosevic insisted that they were necessary to protect Bosnian Serbs from possible Muslim attack.

With no established army and no military tradition, Bosnia was far from being the aggressor that the Serbs played it up to be. In fact, Bosnians were totally unprepared for war. A year before, local defense forces had turned in their weapons at the demand of the federal government, and the UN arms embargo prevented new shipments of weapons into the country. Bosnian Muslims—the most numerous ethnic group in the republic—were craftspeople, teachers, doctors, and small business owners, not soldiers. Many were convinced that their civilized country would never succumb to the insanity of war.

As ethnic tension escalated, Croatia and Slovenia declared their independence from Yugoslavia in 1991. Here, Croatians seek safety in an underground bomb shelter after fighting broke out between the Serbs and Croats.

Other Bosnians were not so sure, however. They had noticed signs that indicated sinister intentions on the part of Bosnian Serbs. For instance, the Sestovics, a Muslim family, noted that they had been excluded from meetings called by Serbs in their apartment building. Serbs taunted them daily by singing nationalist songs. The Sestovics' son had seen Serbs collecting weapons from a delivery truck in town.

Ibro Memisevic, another Bosnian, recalled, "Only the Serbs of Vlasenica were invited to take part [in Yugoslavia People's Army maneuvers], while Muslims were excluded. The atmosphere was being prepared."[38]

"You could feel the war coming," observed Pero Popovic, a Bosnian Serb.[39]

Ethnic Cleansing

War began in Bosnia just days after its citizens declared their independence from Yugoslavia in early March 1992. Serbs struck with the speed and ferocity of a hurricane. Branka Magas, author of *The Destruction of Yugoslavia*, wrote:

Whereas in Croatia the war gradually built up from local Serb "uprisings" in the summer of 1990 to a full-scale war in the summer of 1991, Serbia's aggression against Bosnia-Herzegovina took the form of a blitzkrieg. In Croatia, "ethnic cleansing" was to produce some 300,000 refugees in the course of one and a half years; in Bosnia, the victims of the same policy . . . numbered almost two million within six months.[40]

"Ethnic cleansing" was the term used by the world to describe the Serb tactic of eliminating enemies from regions they had conquered. Many called the process genocide, the systematic killing or harming of members of a national, ethnic, racial, or religious group with the obvious intent of destroying it. The International Genocide Convention, drawn up by the UN in 1948, made genocide an international crime, with perpetrators liable to be charged with war crimes. After witnessing the "cleansing" in Bosnia, Holocaust survivor Simon Wiesenthal pronounced, "Genocide has many forms. You don't have to kill everyone to have genocide. This is genocide, absolutely." [41]

Whether through the use of torture, mass murder, or driving thousands out of their homes and out of their towns, the process of ethnic cleansing was as merciless as it was brutal. "They encircled the place and cut off communications," said Nijaz Rustemovic, a Muslim who watched the destruction of Turalici in eastern Bosnia in 1992. "They went door to door and expelled the people who hadn't already fled. Then they spilled oil all around and lit the village on fire." [42]

Serb federal forces under orders of President Milosevic had joined Bosnian Serb nationalists led by Radovan Karadzic, a psychiatrist turned politician who seemed bent

The damaged area below is in Sarajevo's Muslim quarter. According to author Branka Magas, "Serbia's aggression against Bosnia-Herzegovina took the form of a blitzkrieg."

on gaining power at any price. Together, using the superior weapons of the YPA, they attacked towns and villages across Bosnia. Serbs that did not take part were often drafted by the Serb military and forced to fight. The goal was to destroy anything that represented Muslim or Turkish influence, to encourage non-Serbs to leave permanently, and to clear the way for Serbs to take over the region.

"Our clear impression is that they are not destroying some historical monuments but every historical monument that represents the culture, tradition, and continuity of a people," stated Zehrid Ropic, a Bosnian architect who kept a list of destroyed monuments in northeastern Bosnia.[43]

Not only were buildings destroyed. Everywhere, Muslims were subjected to humiliation and abuse. A 1992 *Time* magazine article reports:

Abdulrahman, 26, a Bosnian Muslim who fled from Zvornik, describes how he and two friends were on their way to the bakery to buy bread when they were nabbed by Serbian soldiers of the federal army and subjected to a night of abuse. Threatened with beatings, they were forced to kneel, butt their heads against a wall and sing songs [insulting to] Muslim women. "We sang," he says, "but they beat us anyway."[44]

The conflict in Bosnia is unique in that the Serbs have waged war, not simply in the battlefield, but against every man, woman, and child who live in Bosnia. Serbs insist that this is not so. They claim that most refugees have voluntarily left their homes to escape the usual hardships of war. They claim that the people held in camps across the country are soldiers who have been legitimately captured during battle.

The war in Bosnia affects every man, woman, and child. This three-year-old girl was wounded in a mortar attack that left her parents dead. Because medical supplies were unavailable, she was operated on without anesthesia.

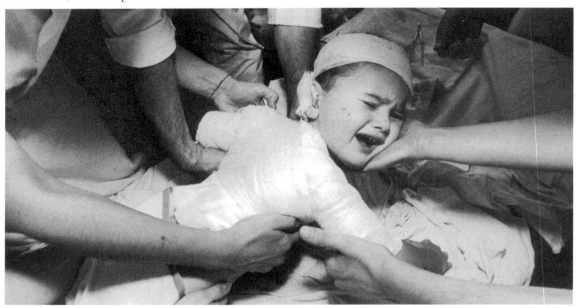

Thousands of Muslims lived in northwest Bosnia before the war. In just a few months, however, they were gone, leaving behind ghost towns such as the one journalist Lara Marlowe describes in a Time *article, "'Cleansed' Wound."*

"In the green meadows and pine forests around Kozarac and Prijedor, stands of poplars, apple and plum orchards, haystacks and fields of unharvested corn and sunflowers evoke a peaceful pastoral dream. But along the road to Prijedor, a burned-out house suddenly appears around a bend. Then more follow, and more, maybe a thousand in all, relics of two-story, white-washed villas with broken red tile roofs. Windows are smashed, walls blackened by smoke. There are no shrapnel and bullet holes recording some battle here; this is what 'ethnic cleansing' looks like a day or even an hour later. Laundry still hangs on clotheslines, a sign of how quickly disaster fell upon the inhabitants. Only one house remains intact, the home of a Serb couple who sit drinking their morning coffee on the balcony, their mattresses airing in the sunshine."

Evidence to the contrary is only too obvious. A majority of both refugees and captives are civilians. One man says, "Among the prisoners there were women and old men, men of over 60 and one who was 73. Prisoners were not being brought from the battlefields as captives but from their homes."[45]

Thousands of refugees and prisoners also testify that they had been forced to abandon their homes at gunpoint. In 1994, one older refugee, recovering from a broken hip, had been severely beaten and tortured in her own living room. In the process her hip was rebroken. Then soldiers—in this case Croats—forced her onto the street and confiscated her property.

Inhumane Treatment

The cost of ethnic cleansing has been extremely high for its victims. Most have been forced to sign away their land, their homes, and their possessions and promise never to return. Many were then marched to nearby towns where they were herded into make-do camps—auditoriums, sports stadiums, and schools—and left to survive as best they could. Others were put on buses and trains and sent out of the country.

Transport itself was often torture. In many cases reported in 1992, refugees clutching children and a duffel bag or two were ordered into freight cars, which were then sealed and sent to various locales. Refugees were sometimes trapped inside for days. Conditions were unbearable.

"There was no food, no water and no fresh air," reported Began Fazlic, a refugee who survived one such journey. "There was no toilet, just holes in the floor." Uncounted numbers of people died during these ordeals. "Most of the dead were children," said Fazlic. "They'd open the door, take the bodies out and dump them by the roadside. We weren't allowed to bury them."[46]

Despite confirmed reports of inhumane treatment, Serb officials denied responsibility for any such incidents. "None of the refugees asked for first-class carriages," explained

Ethnic cleansing in Bosnia resulted in thousands of men, women, and children losing their homes and being herded to refugee camps aboard crowded buses or trains.

Stojan Zupljanin, police chief of Banja Luka, a northern Bosnian city through which the trains passed in 1992. "None of them said, 'If you don't have a passenger train, I wouldn't go.' Anything is better than walking."[47]

"Good-Bye to the World"

As brutal as these incidents appeared, some captives endured more savage treatment. For men, beatings were routine. One victim reported, "We were beaten with iron bars, baseball bats, and truncheons. . . . I have watched baseball on TV, and they swung [the bats] as if they were hitting a ball, with both hands. That night I said good-bye to the world. I just wanted to die."[48]

Many did die. Witnesses testified that a great number of mass murders took place throughout the country in the first months of the war. Prisoners were often stabbed and beaten to death. Some were burned alive. Hundreds were shot, then their bodies were carelessly dumped into ravines or rivers.

The fate of those not murdered was equally grim. One Serb soldier reported plans for the captives he guarded. "We won't waste our bullets on them," he said. "They have no roof. There is sun and rain, cold nights, and beatings two times a day. We give them no food and no water. They will starve like animals."[49]

Rape as a Weapon

While Muslim men suffered starvation, torture, and death, Muslim women and girls were experiencing a different kind of torment. Relief workers calculated that at least twenty thousand had been raped by Serbs between the beginning of the war and the end of 1992. Often, whole villages of women had been rounded up and subjected to this abuse.

Although rape has been traditionally recognized as a part of war, a kind of perverted payback for soldiers' suffering during battle, in Bosnia rape was committed as a deliberate tactic. "We have orders to rape the girls," one soldier told his victim.[50] Many men have claimed they were reluctant to commit rape, and said they had given in to pressure from their leaders and their comrades.

Serbs are well aware of the terrible connotations rape carries for Muslims. Women not only are traumatized by the act, they view it as an unspeakable horror that affects themselves, their families, and their entire race. Rape by a Serb is both shameful and degrading because it is seen as a violation of ethnic purity. It causes tremendous guilt, since Muslim men blame themselves for not being able to protect their women. It also produces family conflict. Men sometimes perversely blame their wives for being a part of the act.

"Everyone who is with us now (other refugees) does not believe we were forced," explained Sevlata Ajanovic, who was raped

Serbian POWs exhume the corpses of one hundred slain Muslims. Their mass grave was discovered in September 1992 outside Mostar in Bosnia.

repeatedly after being captured by Serbs in 1992. "And they think we are going to go with them (the Serbs) again. We can't imagine marriage as a normal thing. We know that the man will always be suspicious."[51]

For Muslim women, rape was a final and permanent humiliation. Seen through the eyes of their religion and their culture, they could never be the same again.

No Outside Help

As war overtook them and tore their country apart, the Bosnian government scrambled to put together an army that it hoped could at least save Sarajevo, the country's capital, from being overrun by Serb forces.

Though willing, the untrained volunteers were a shaky defense, and most Bosnians believed that the world would rush to help them when it became widely known how unfair the fight was. Yet time passed, thousands died, and world leaders did little but encourage peace talks and deplore the violence. Without exception, they hesitated to use force against the Serbs.

There were a number of reasons for that hesitation in the first year of the war. Germany was prevented by its constitution from going to war. Britain and France worried that if they got involved, the UN peacekeeping forces they had already sent to Bosnia and Croatia would be killed or held hostage. The United States was unwilling to commit troops and money to a conflict that might not easily be won. It could not forget the Vietnam War.

Lack of military intervention outraged and bewildered Bosnia's defenders. They pointed out the obvious parallels between Bosnia and events leading up to the Holocaust, events that the world had promised to never let happen again. Yet those events were happening. By June 1992, less than two

As war tore their country apart, the government desperately put together an army of Bosnian defenders. Willing to risk their lives for their homeland, Bosnian soldiers dart past a known Serbian sniper position.

Murder at Ugar Gorge

Semir K., a Bosnian Muslim, will never forget the day he was unlucky enough to be picked up by Serb police near his hometown of Carakovo. His eyewitness account of the massacre of two hundred Muslims that followed appears in a Time *magazine article entitled "Murder at Ugar Gorge."*

"After half an hour, we stopped. It was very quiet. Then a soldier came in and pointed to a man at the front [of the bus] and said, 'You.' They got out, and we heard a single shot. Then another Serb came in and said to the soldier on board, 'Now get two out.' More shots. Then we realized it was over, there was no life for us. They started taking people by threes, and we heard machine-gun bursts along with pistol shots. . . .

I had already decided to run, whatever happened. I pushed the soldier at the backdoor slightly; three steps was all I needed to jump into the gorge. I landed in a tree, lost my breath completely. . . . I was lying on my back and could see what they were doing up there. I watched them sling the bodies into the canyon; it all took about an hour. . . .

I spent two nights and two days in the river, walking but mostly swimming. . . . By the sixth day, I was very hungry, but the thirst was even worse. I was coming to a settlement but didn't know what kind. . . . I heard young girls passing; one of them cried, 'Mehmet [an Islamic given name], coffee is ready.' A stone fell from my heart; they were Muslims. . . . They took me in."

months after fighting began, over twelve thousand people were dead. Tens of thousands were missing and wounded. Over 1.5 million had been expelled from their homes.

And, just as world leaders had tried to pacify Hitler when he invaded Czechoslovakia before World War II, the world was appeasing the Serbs, promising them land in return for peace. Just as Hitler had taken advantage of the world's weakness, so were the Serbs pressing their advantage, driving Bosnia to its knees.

"Bosnia-Herzegovina Has Ceased to Exist"

Desperately, the Bosnian government begged the West to at least lift the arms embargo that gave Serbs, with their vast federal arsenal, a strong advantage in the fighting. "We do not need a single Western soldier to come here and fight for our freedom. We just ask for the right to defend ourselves," said one Bosnian commander in late 1992.[52]

World leaders, afraid that additional weapons would only prolong the fight, refused. In their eyes, the war was all but over. Serbs had captured more than two-thirds of the country. The Bosnian government was all but powerless. It had no choice but to surrender. "Bosnia-Herzegovina has ceased to exist," a senior British diplomat stated in July 1992, only three months after the beginning of the war.[53]

Loyal Bosnians did not listen to the predictions. Despite their weak position, they continued to fight. Their lives, their homeland, and their future were at stake.

Neighbor Against Neighbor

As war tore their country apart, ordinary Bosnians struggled to understand what was happening. One Bosnian Muslim spoke for his people when he said:

> When I think back now, . . . I am haunted by questions: Why? How? Why did it happen? How could neighbor turn against neighbor, friend against friend, relative against relative? In Bosnia-Hercegovina we are so intermingled that there is hardly a single family which does not number Muslims, Serbs, and Croats among its members.[54]

Vahida Kartal, a Muslim from Osave in eastern Bosnia, had grown up surrounded by Serb neighbors. For the first year of the war, she and her family believed that all would be well. Then, everything began to change.

"Our Serbian friends assured us they would protect us. But after that the occasional killing and regular theft started," she explained. Soon Vahida's Serb neighbors thought nothing of walking into the Kartal home and taking the television or anything else of value. Then a local Serb murdered his Muslim neighbor. Finally the entire Kartal family was taken away to a refugee camp. "They want to make their own republic and they don't want to live with us," Vahida said.[55]

Life, which had once been so pleasant, had become a confusing and dangerous affair. With little warning, millions of Bosni-

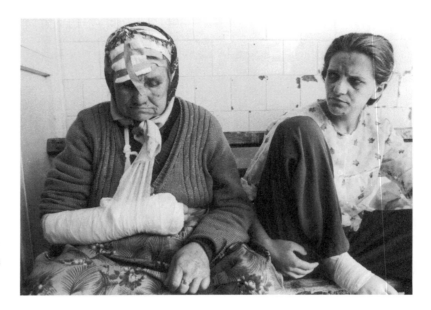

As war continued and neighbor turned against neighbor, life in Bosnia meant constant danger. These women were injured during shelling in Travnik, Bosnia.

ans were plunged into a nightmare from which there seemed to be no escape.

Living with the Enemy

Before the war, most Bosnians had been tolerant of one another's differences. Muslims, Croats, and Serbs shopped in the same stores, lived in the same neighborhoods, and helped each other through difficult times.

It was also a common practice in Bosnia for members of different ethnic groups to intermarry. Across the country, almost a third of all marriages were mixed. "We were brought up not to think about religion and nationality," explained Misha, a Muslim woman married to a Serb businessman. "It was perfectly acceptable to think of ourselves as Yugoslavs."[56]

As war swept the country, however, much of that tolerance was forgotten. Couples from mixed backgrounds faced unexpected prejudice—neighbors became hostile, families critical, and employers discriminatory. People like Misha and her husband remained loyal to each other even when both became outcasts in their own neighborhood. In other instances, however, marriages ended in separation. In one Croatian city in 1991, officials estimated that seven out of ten divorces could be traced to problems that developed within mixed marriages because of ethnic tensions.

Caught in the Middle

Children who were products of these mixed families faced even greater challenges. "We're neither Muslim, nor Croat, nor Serb," explained a young woman doctor of Croat and Serb parents.[57]

Many young people, shaken by a society torn apart by ethnic tension, felt confused and rebellious because of this mixed heritage. In one case, a Serb teen with a Croat grandfather wanted to "release one quarter of the Croatian blood from her body so she could become pure Serb." In another, a thirteen-year-old boy with a Serb father and a Croat mother chose to identify himself as Croat. "My son was troubled because I am a Serb," explained his father. "I told him I was the father he had known all his life."[58]

Life as a Second-Class Citizen

As friends turned on each other, and families split apart, in some parts of the country non-Serbs tried to protect themselves and save their possessions by appeasing their Serb neighbors.

"We made a deal with the Serbian authorities," explained one villager. "We fly white flags on our houses as a sign of our loyalty. We will not oppose them, and they will not harm us. So far, they have kept their word, but we don't know about the future."[59]

The future was not bright in most cases. In the best of circumstances, Muslims were barely tolerated. In towns such as Banja Luka and Celinac, those who remained were required to follow "special status" decrees. These decrees, chillingly similar to those imposed on Jews during the Nazi era in Europe, set strict curfews for all non-Serbs and forbade many apparently normal activities such as fishing, hunting, driving a car, and gathering in groups of more than three.

Despite efforts to abide by the new rules, Muslim "lawbreakers" were often persecuted, arrested, even killed. Most became second-class citizens, deprived of their rights, their jobs, and their security. Journalist Anna

Husarska reported on her visit to Banja Luka in 1992:

> Everyone I met in Merhamet [Banja Luka's Muslim office of humanitarian aid] had been fired: lawyers, doctors, clerks, tailors. None would give his name. Their stories were similar: one said his neighbor, a 35-year-old taxi driver, had been killed in the night; one said his brother had been taken to the Manjaca detention camp; the aunt of another had her house taken away during her absence.[60]

Many families found it easier to leave than to cope with the humiliation and threats they had to endure.

Life as a Refugee

Some who fled were lucky enough to escape to sympathetic countries such as Hungary or Germany, where they could find jobs and begin life over again. Others ended up in refugee camps set up by humanitarian organizations such as the Red Cross or by local officials who could offer a stadium or other large building as shelter. There the refugees lived, sometimes for months, until they could transfer to more permanent quarters.

In most cases, life in these camps was relatively safe, but primitive and demeaning to people used to hot water and indoor plumbing. Many lived in tents. Water had to be carried from outside faucets and heated over a small oil or wood stove if it was heated at all. Bathing was a luxury; toilets were public and located a good distance away.

Privacy was impossible. In a typical camp in Croatia in 1993, ten to fifteen people shared one tiny room in a dormitory-style barrack. In

Forced out of their home, a mother and her small child live in a refugee center while awaiting acceptance by another country.

the cold months, even indoors was chilly—newly washed clothes draped between beds sometimes froze before they dried. Cooking was prohibited, although the rule was often ignored. Food was provided by relief agencies.

The refugees had some things to be thankful for, however. They were alive. They had blankets and a roof over their heads. Still, there was little to do but talk and wait, either for loved ones who were missing, or for a chance to get out of the area and start over again.

Returning home was out of the question. Moving to another country often required identity papers such as passports and visas, and those had been left behind in the confusion of Serb onslaughts. Unwanted and unprotected, the refugees had become people without a country.

Life in Concentration Camps

Bosnians in refugee camps were lucky compared to the thousands of people who were sent to Serb-run concentration camps—sometimes known as death camps—that were set up across the country in the first year of the war. There, overcrowding, filth, and the torment of heat, cold, dysentery, and lice were the best that prisoners could hope for. At worst, conditions were extremely brutal. Lengthy beatings were daily events. Guards devised terrible mental and physical tortures that often set prisoner against prisoner and broke the wills of the strongest men.

In the Susica camp, a former military depot in eastern Bosnia, hundreds of men, women, and children lived crammed together into sheds too small to hold them. "The place was full of other civilians," said one former prisoner. "Some were wounded, some very dirty. There was a concrete floor, and virtually nowhere to sit."[61]

Mass murders were common at Susica, much as they were at other such camps in 1992. One guard testified that he personally witnessed at least three thousand killings in the four months the camp was open. Many prisoners who were not shot or beaten to death starved. Daily rations were nothing more than weak tea, a cup of thin soup, and a piece of bread. Often twenty to thirty people divided one loaf.

Special Status

On a visit to Bosnia in the summer of 1992, journalist Anna Husarska was able to obtain one of the "special status" decrees that were issued in towns such as Celinac. These decrees, which she wrote about in the article "City of Fear," published in the New Republic *magazine, imposed restrictions on all non-Serbs in the region.*

"'Due to military actions in Celinac,' the document declares, all non-Serbs are given a 'special status.' In addition to a 4 PM to 6 AM curfew, non-Serbs are forbidden to:
—meet in cafes, restaurants, or other public places
—bathe or swim in the Vrbanija or Josavka rivers
—hunt or fish
—move to another town without authorization
—carry a weapon
—drive or travel by car
—gather in groups of more than three men
—contact relatives from outside Celinac (all household visits must be reported)
—use means of communication other than the post office phone
—wear uniforms: military, police, or forest guard
—sell real estate or exchange homes without approval."

Freedom to move about the camp was limited, even though there was little chance that prisoners would escape. The camps were encircled by multiple rows of barbed wire fence and watched over by guards and sometimes dogs. Prisoners, weak from hunger, did little but stand or lie on the ground for weeks at a time. As one of the milder forms of torture, Serb guards sometimes required all to stand for twenty-four hours at a stretch.

In Manjaca camp in northern Bosnia, conditions were equally inhumane. While suffering abuse and starvation, prisoners there were also forced to work for their captors. Camp survivor Orhan Bosnevic (a pseudonym to protect his relatives still living in Bosnia) remembered his stay at Manjaca:

> The camp inmates sometimes worked in the prison workshop or outside. Making pistol and rifle butts, digging ditches, forestry work. They were also building a church: the mosque in Kljuc had had its roof stripped, and now persons from a concentration camp were putting it on a church. One team of inmates was building a boat for. . . the camp commandant.[62]

No One Left to Kill

Omarska, a former iron mine in northwest Bosnia, was the site of one of the largest of the concentration camps, holding an estimated eleven thousand prisoners. Survivors claimed that more than a thousand Muslims and Croats had been locked into cramped metal cages, without sanitary facilities, adequate food, or exercise. Many were kicked, burned, and slashed with knives. Hundreds had been shot; others disappeared, never to be heard of again. Some of the prisoners had been identified as political leaders and well-

to-do persons who had lived in the region around Omarska, although most people fitting these descriptions had been executed to ensure that Bosnian leadership would be permanently weakened.

After outside authorities demanded that the Red Cross be allowed to enter such concentration camps in the summer of 1992 to investigate conditions there, Serbs made improvements, shifted prisoners to new locations, and shut some of the camps down. Omarska and Susica were two of them.

Susica closed simply because it was no longer needed. "There were no more Muslims in the . . . area," admitted one Serb who had served as a guard in Susica.[63] All had been killed or deported.

Life in the Trenches

Although thousands of helpless Bosnians put up little resistance as they were pushed out of their homes and into the camps, some loyal Bosnians—men and boys armed with whatever weapons they could find—joined the newly formed Bosnian government army, dug into the hills, and fought head to head with the Serbs.

Few of the fighters on either side had been formally trained to take part in battle. Some Serbs were members of the federal Yugoslav army, but, for the most part, troops were farmers, laborers, teachers, and businessmen who turned out to fight.

Not surprisingly, both Bosnian and Serb armies were sometimes unconventional and informal in structure. Especially in the case of Bosnian Serb nationalists, many combat units were not part of a chain of command. Each unit had its own leader, and often the soldiers themselves decided on a plan of action. For instance, Ljuba Mikerevic, whose

Parents grieve over the body of their fifteen-year-old son, a Bosnian combatant killed in the fighting. The Bosnian army consists of men and even boys unaccustomed to war—students, farmers, teachers, and businessmen.

unit was stationed only two miles from his hometown in 1992, walked home once a week to make sure his wife and two young daughters were still alive and had food. He and other men with families in the area declared that they would refuse to leave if their unit was ordered to another region.

"I am willing to listen," said one fighter, speaking of the orders he was given by his commanding officer, "but I decide in the end."[64]

"Not Afraid to Die"

Like millions of other men throughout recent history, soldiers on all sides of the war endured hardship, loneliness, and danger as they fought for the cause they believed in. In summer heat and winter cold, many crouched in trenches, rough shelters, or bombed-out buildings, waiting for a signal to attack the enemy. Their surroundings were often muddy and littered with cigarette butts and spent cartridges. In the hills, shelters were cobbled together from dirt-filled cartridge boxes and loose boards.

"We have the basics here," said one Serb fighter. "We have food, cigarettes, a little money and our tank. It is enough. We can fight alone if we have to. We are not afraid to die."[65]

After Muslims and Croats in contested areas of Bosnia had been killed or driven away, Serb soldiers often moved into their homes, taking advantage of the comfort they

A young Bosnian electrician-turned-sniper takes aim at a Serbian soldier. Although untrained and ill equipped for war, Bosnian troops fought valiantly to save their lives and their country.

offered. Few had pity to waste on the former owners.

"Their name was Fazlic," said Dragan Zamaklaar, a Serb who had appropriated a Muslim home and lived there with his fellow soldiers in 1992. "They left some furniture, and we found a few of their family snapshots. I didn't even bother to look at them."[66]

"Fighting for our Future"

Those who fought on the side of the Bosnian government were less complacent. They had not wanted war in the first place, and they were outgunned by Serb heavy weapons. "We were fighting with rifles against tanks," said one leader, whose men were driven back from the positions they had held in 1992. "If

we'd had one-tenth of what the Serbs had, we could have stayed."[67]

Still, Bosnian troops were motivated to fight hard. Their lives and the lives of their families were at stake. Pavle, a Muslim civilian fighting in Sarajevo, described his feelings in a 1992 letter to his wife, whom he had sent out of the country early in the war:

I stay alert in the mud-filled trench to avoid being killed, and we are being constantly fired at with every kind of weapon of every conceivable calibre. . . . I shoot at people I do not hate, I shoot at them only because they shoot at me intending to kill me. . . . We are doing this as if it were any other job. We try to do it to the best of our ability and to stay alive and so far it has gone well. I am neither a hero nor a coward. I am fighting simply because it is demanded of me at the moment. I am comforted by the thought that I am fighting for our future.[68]

Living Under Siege

In towns and cities such as Sarajevo where citizens chose to resist rather than surrender, the Serbs often utilized a siege strategy, which involved cutting off all transportation, communication, and supply lines into and out of the area. Their goal was to starve and demoralize residents until they died or were willing to leave the country.

Srebrenica, a town in eastern Bosnia, came under siege in early 1993. For months on end, people there remained isolated from the outside world, with no electricity and little food, water, or clothing. Aid was provided by the few truck convoys of food that Serb patrols allowed through their blockades. In the winter, thousands of ragged, hungry refugees who had been driven down from surrounding villages filled every available facility to the bursting point.

"We were living in a room that was the size of a toilet stall. My [seventeen-year-old] son and I had one bed, and it had no legs," said Rasim Ganic, a Muslim refugee.[69] Those without shelter slept in the snow in winter and scavenged in garbage cans for food scraps.

Worn down by starvation, cold, and fear, many people became frantic to escape their captivity. Opportunities to leave were few and sometimes ended in tragedy. When UN rescue trucks arrived in Srebrenica in 1993 to carry the neediest people to safety, desperate citizens stormed aboard, trampling weaker women and children. During the eight-hour trip to safety, at least five children and two women died.

Desperate Lives

Journalist Lyn Cryderman published his article "In the Camps . . .", in Christianity Today, *after a visit to the former Yugoslavia in early 1993.*

"I have been to refugee camps, but none like Gasinci in western Croatia. Winter has arrived, and at least half the camp's population is living in crude, military tents.

There are no floors; no water—except a well a half-kilometer away; rats as big as small cats. With temperatures dropping, the race to cut and store wood consumes every able body. . . .

Three children follow me everywhere. One reaches for my hand whenever I am not taking pictures. Later, an interpreter tells me I remind them of their father. He was dragged from their house in a Bosnian village and shot in front of his wife and children. Their mother was dragged away by teenage soldiers smelling of *sljivoic*, the potent brandy passed around each morning to keep the troops from thinking too much about their deeds.

It is time to leave. And as I bend to receive my gift of two slender arms hugging my neck, I think of my own little Molly, wondering why one child should sleep in down and cotton, another child in a tent with rats."

"They were alive when we passed Edrinjaca," cried Hanifa Hajdarovic, mother of two of the children who had died. "But there was a jolt, I was knocked down, and my children were both crushed. We thought we would be safe if we left Srebrenica."[70]

The "White Death"

People in Gorazde also faced hunger, cold, and deprivation as Serbs encircled their town, then shelled it for weeks on end in 1993. Fatima Malokos, who had lived through both world wars, commented, "In World War I they only fought, in the second they only burned some houses. In this one they just shell civilians. This one is the worst."[71]

To obtain food and supplies, some of the strongest citizens braved sniper fire and the "white death"—an overpowering sleepiness that tempted the exhausted to lie down in the snow—on a nightly walk sixty miles through mountain passes in subfreezing temperatures. Numerous volunteers, weakened by starvation and cold, were found frozen to death along the snowy track.

Those who survived obtained supplies such as flour and cooking oil provided by relief workers at the other end of the route. In mid-1993, however, passage along the mountain course was cut off by Serb guns.

Desperate to escape besieged Srebrenica, Muslims storm aboard an overloaded UN rescue truck.

Death Camp

At least ninety-four concentration camps were known to be scattered throughout Bosnia in 1992. Although some closed, relief workers guess that many still remain. Orhan Bosnevic (his name was changed to protect relatives still in Bosnia) was a survivor of Manjaca, one of the worst. His experiences are related in the book Why Bosnia?

"After the beatings and the hunger, our biggest problems were lack of fresh air, water, and hygiene. Suffocation [due to overcrowding] and thirst had already killed some of us. As for hygiene, it was virtually non-existent. Our heads were shaved immediately on arrival, and I had two baths of two or three minutes each during my whole imprisonment. . . .

Field latrines had been dug between the sheds. When it rained, the contents overflowed into the sheds, for the ground was sloping. . . . The all pervading filth meant that we all had cold sores and dysentery. Later we managed to get a little water, contaminated with diesel fuel, from a nearby lake where the vehicles were washed. Then we were able, after a fashion, to wash our clothes.

We did our washing at the back of the sheds, next to the minefield. Once, when I was inside the shed, there was a massive explosion, followed a few seconds later by the thud of something black hitting one of the transparent roof panels. A murmur went round the shed: 'Another man gone.'"

The besieged civilians were then on their own, except for rare convoys of aid that Serbs occasionally allowed into the town.

Living Without Laughter

As living conditions grew increasingly desperate in Bosnia, those who remained realized that they would have to rely on their own determination and strength if they were to survive. No one understood that better than the people of Sarajevo. For years—since May 1992—the people of the capital city lived in a continual state of siege, cut off from the outside world, resisting the enemy when everyone predicted that the struggle was hopeless.

Zlatko Dizdarevic, an editor at *Oslobodenje*, the last surviving newspaper in Sarajevo, described the terrible effect the war has had on Sarajevans:

If there are any traces of smiles left on our faces after all this, they surely must be the smiles of idiots, smiles that mean absolutely nothing since true laughter does not live among us anymore. . . . [Sarajevo has] become a ghetto with its own logic, its own laws, its own morality and its own imagination. And of course, its own malice, intolerance and nastiness.[72]

The city had become an enormous concentration camp, and the Sarajevans were its prisoners.

Sarajevo Under Siege

Sarajevo is certainly not the only Bosnian city to endure the agony of war. But, in the eyes of its people and the world, its suffering symbolizes the madness that has been let loose in that country. Before the war, Sarajevans, even more than other Bosnians, were known for their tolerance, their love of peace, and their horror of violence. Almost 50 percent of Sarajevans were married to someone from a different ethnic group. Journalist Anna Husarska found that some would not even speak of their ethnic origins. "They all identify themselves as 'Bosnian,'" she explained.[73]

Sarajevans saw themselves as highly civilized people, who solved problems through discussion and compromise, rather than force. For them, war was as immoral as it was incomprehensible. Bosnian Aziz Hadzihasanovic, an official of the former Republic of Yugoslavia, wrote:

> I am ashamed of being present at a time and a place . . . where, at the end of the twentieth century and upon European territory, children are killed with precision rifles, innocent men with mortars, where aeroplanes are dropping bombs and where, to put it briefly, every living thing, everything human and everything that exists is being destroyed with the utmost brutality.[74]

The city of Sarajevo was something of a cosmopolitan center, much like the European cities of Rome, Paris, and London. According to journalist Roy Gutman, "It was a place of learning and of commerce, a westward-looking city in an exotic setting."[75] Art colonies, theaters, museums—Sarajevo had them all. It also boasted a university and many fine libraries, among them the National Library with thousands of historical volumes. Young Sarajevans could go out to nightclubs and discos with their friends. Families could enjoy the latest American films by Disney and Steven Spielberg, or classic ballet productions such as *Swan Lake* put on by the Sarajevo Ballet Company.

Sarajevan Hospitality

The world had heard of Sarajevo as well, even before the war in Bosnia. In 1984, the 14th Winter Olympics had been held there. Local firms and volunteers had proudly prepared the sites necessary for the games: a stadium large enough to hold opening activities, a sports complex for skating, two Olympic villages where athletes and coaches ate and slept. In the heart of Sarajevo, a new Holiday Inn was built to help house some of the spectators who poured into the city for the big event.

During the course of the games, happy celebrants enjoyed the hospitality of the region. They learned about native foods such as *rahatloukoum* (Turkish Delight) and *cevapi* (Yugoslav meatballs). They drank coffee in the

Sarajevo during happier times, when the city hosted the 14th Winter Olympics in 1984.

cobblestoned marketplace. They explored Old Town with its narrow streets and Turkish bazaars. No one imagined that, less than ten years later, the same streets would be veritable death traps for those who dared travel them.

"Let This Be a Warning"

The first shots of the war were fired in Sarajevo in early March 1992, only days after Bosnian Muslims and Croats had voted for Bosnia-Hercegovina to become an independent nation (Bosnian Serbs boycotted the vote). On March 3, Serbs wearing ski masks and carrying guns set up barricades around Muslim portions of the city. "We are not going to accept an independent Bosnia-Herzegovina," stated Radovan Karadzic, the Bosnian Serb leader. "Let this be a warning."[76]

Sarajevans resisted the takeover. Refusing to fight but willing to take a stand, many citizens organized a pro-independence march through the town, chanting, "Down with the barricades, we are unarmed."[77]

But the city had already been surrounded by Serb artillery. Serb forces—from the Serbian republic as well as nationalist Bosnian Serbs—had stationed themselves in the hills around the city. They brought with them a variety of weapons—tanks, mortars, automatic rifles with telescopic sights. By May 1, 1992, the capital was being shelled around the clock. The battle for Sarajevo had begun.

Under the Guns

The war is an ever-present fact of life to the people of Bosnia. In an article in Christianity Today, *journalist Lyn Cryderman reveals that anyone in Sarajevo could enter the thick of the fighting simply by stepping out of doors.*

"I head across the street behind [my] hotel. Every building shows the effects of direct, heavy-artillery hits, and small arms fire punctuates the air. I am very scared. Two women walk past me and I rush to keep up with them.

'Do you live here?' is my first stupid question.

'Yes, about three kilometers from here.'

'Isn't it dangerous to walk home?'

The first woman says it isn't, but the second corrects her. 'Yes, it is very dangerous, but we can't think about it. If we did, we would never leave our homes. We are trying to live normal lives, but it is very difficult.'

I ask her if she is Muslim.

'No, I am Christian, but I am Bosnian. The chetniks (a derisive term for the Serbian irregulars) won't ask. They will kill all of us.'

'But we hear that the Serbs want to remove only the Muslims.'

'They want Sarajevo. And Banja Luka. And Vukovich. They want everything.'

We are about five blocks from the hotel and seem to be closer to the gunfire I had heard earlier. I feel like a wimp because I do not want to go any farther. When I stop, they stop too.

'It is not good to stand still,' one of them remarks.

'I think I will go back to the hotel,' I respond.

'You are an American?'

I nod."

Destroying a Way of Life

Not all Serbs in Sarajevo or in Bosnia were nationalists or Milosevic sympathizers. During the war, a great number fought side by side with Muslims and Bosnian Croats. Close to eighty thousand Serbs were part of the Bosnian government force in Sarajevo. They were willing to die to preserve the multicultural society in which they believed.

Nationalist Serbs, however, were just as dedicated in their efforts to cleanse Bosnia. In Sarajevo, as in other urban areas, that meant breaking down the order and structure of the city. Government buildings were bombed, as were hospitals and centers for communication and transportation. Mosques and churches turned to rubble almost overnight. The hundred-year-old city hall, the parliament building, the main post office, and the train station were also targets of attack. One Bosnian described the sweeping destruction:

> At night I watched the fiery trails of the grenades as they screamed overhead on their way to destroy all the trams and buses of the public transport services. Then they hit the milk distribution centre, the maternity hospital and the "Vijecnica," our great, beautiful library where a hundred thousand volumes were reduced to cinders.[78]

No Power, No Water, No Heat

During the course of the war, the Serb army concentrated on destroying every essential of life in Sarajevo, beginning by disrupting the utility systems. With the first mortar fire, electric lines were cut. Water and gas mains were broken. Zlatko Dizdarevic wrote:

> For days there has been no running water. It rained yesterday, but many of us didn't think to collect the water in pots and buckets. How would we think of collecting rainwater, after so many years in which water ran from the tap? But the next time it rains, if it does, we'll know what to do.[79]

Utilities were erratically shut off and turned on, depending on the frequency of Serb attack and the skill of crews who repeatedly risked their lives to repair the damage. Residents quickly learned to hoard water, to go to bed when darkness fell, to cook when electricity was available. During long periods without water, residents went out in search of a pipe or spring where it might be found. The search could take hours, and to bring home a few jugs took a great deal of effort. Sarajevans were creative when it came to devising ways to lessen the chore. In her diary, Zlata Filipovic, a young Bosnian girl, recorded some of them:

> You should see the different kinds of water carts they have. How inventive people are.

In Sarajevo, the once beautiful library stands in ruins—testament to the senseless destruction that characterized the siege of Sarajevo.

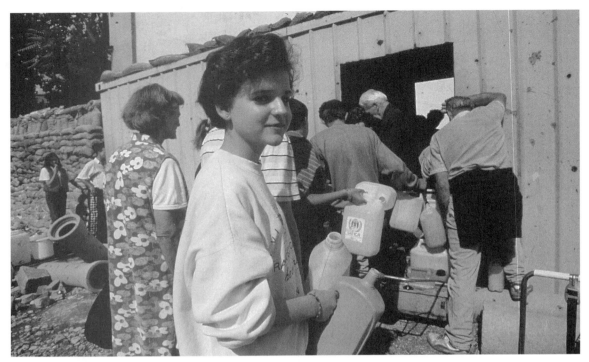

Zlata Filipovic (pictured) kept a diary describing her life in war-ravaged Bosnia. Her entries include comments about finding and collecting water, tasks vital to survival.

Two-wheelers, three-wheelers, . . . wheelchairs, hospital tables, supermarket carts and, topping them all—a sled on roller skates.[80]

Keeping warm during the war was also difficult. Bosnian winters are bitter; snow and below freezing temperatures are common. Most windows broke during the shelling, turning homes without gas and electricity into iceboxes. Many people were able to find or construct some type of wood-burning stove that they installed for cooking and heating. Early on, however, wood became as precious as food and water. Then trees that graced the town's streets, cemeteries, and parks were cut down. By the second winter, even the roots had been dug up and carried away.

Sarajevans then resorted to using furniture, kitchen cabinets, and floorboards as sources of fuel. "I counted all the cupboards in the apartment; there are dozens of them and all made of good heavy oak. They will each last for two days at least," one Sarajevan related to a friend.[81]

"Naked Pasta"

To cut off food and other necessities, the Serbs continually blocked roads and fired at incoming UN airplanes that brought aid to Sarajevo and other urban centers. Soon market shelves stood empty, and people formed long lines in front of bakeries when rumor had it that bread might be available. Plain pasta or rice became the mainstay of most meals. "One's hair stands on end at the thought of sitting down and facing a bowl of the same old 'naked' pasta or rice yet again," wrote one Sarajevan.[82]

Humanitarian aid, food supplied by the UN and other charitable organizations, played an important role in the survival of Sarajevans, as it did for those in other besieged areas. During the harsh Bosnian winters, many people relied almost wholly on such aid, which relief workers managed to fly or truck past Serb guns. At times, supplies were little more than a skimpy package of flour, oil, and cheese. At other times, rations were more generous and varied. Zlata Filipovic described one larger portion of aid:

> On July 8 we got a UN package. Humanitarian aid. Inside were 6 cans of beef, 5 cans of fish, 2 boxes of cheese, 3 kilos of detergent, 5 bars of soap, 2 kilos of sugar and 5 liters of cooking oil. All in all, a super package. But Daddy had to stand in line for four hours to get it.[83]

After months of going without, people naturally yearned for fruits, vegetables, candy, and cigarettes, which they had once taken for granted. Anyone lucky enough to have money could make purchases at the market, but selection was limited, prices were high, and Bosnian dinars, the country's currency, were all but worthless. Some merchants accept nothing but German deutsche marks. At times, a pack of chewing gum might cost six hundred dinars; a bag of candy, one thousand dinars. One woman wrote in 1992, "I haven't got a job; I'm on the waiting list. I get two thousand Bosnian dinars a month and with that I can buy half a kilo of pasta."[84]

In summer, some families grew a few vegetables on balconies or in window boxes.

"You remember that cupboard in the utility room?" one man wrote to his wife. "I emptied it, sowed onions, lettuces, carrots and celery in it and put it by the door on the right. . . . I only hope the balcony won't collapse under the weight."[85] Others modified recipes to use nettles and other weeds that grow in town.

A woman spends Christmas Eve searching for wood in the ruins of downtown Sarajevo in 1992. With no gas or electricity to warm homes during the harsh Bosnian winters, Bosnians rely on wood-burning stoves to provide warmth.

Pazi Snajper

Leaving the semisecurity of home to go to a market or anywhere else was always a daring venture, and in the beginning of the war, careful parents kept children inside for weeks on end. Those who went out encountered disturbing sights at every turn. Streets were littered with burned-out cars. Buildings were blasted and deserted. Bodies sometimes lay on the sidewalk.

The greatest danger came from snipers armed with rifles equipped with telescopic sights who stationed themselves in strategic spots—on hilltops, in empty buildings—and picked off those who came within range. In areas of town where battles were long-term and shelling and sniper fire constant, people starved to death because they could not leave their homes to get supplies.

"For months the children of Dobrinja [a suburb of Sarajevo] have had only sugarless tea to drink, if you can call a concoction of herbs and boiled leaves 'tea,'" wrote Zlatko Dizdarevic in 1992. "The inhabitants break up furniture and floorboards in order to heat

A woman clutches her child as she darts across an intersection targeted by snipers in downtown Sarajevo.

A Bitter Anniversary

Journalist Zlatko Dizdarevic's news articles mapped the progress of the war as they marked the change in the mood and the outlook of Sarajevans over time. This article, published in his book, Sarajevo, A War Journal, *commemorated three bitter months of war.*

"Today, according to our calculations, is an anniversary: one hundred days of solitude. It has been exactly a hundred days since the first shot was fired on a citizen of Sarajevo. . . .

We no longer live in the same places, we don't have the same neighbors. . . . We no longer go to the same bakery or the same newsstand. . . . We no longer switch the light on in our apartments; no longer use our dinner dishes; the piles of plastic water buckets in the hallways and under our beds (if we still have a bed) no longer bother us. We've forgotten what it was like to be irritated by a television commercial. We don't get angry at the mailman for coming late, because there no longer is a mailman. We would give anything in the world just to get a bill, no matter how big or how small, because it would mean that someone believes we're still alive and capable of paying. . . .

A hundred days is nothing. A spring we haven't seen, a winter that is constantly upon us. Nevertheless, these hundred days are engraved in our memories as if they had been a hundred years."

their apartments, and then handfuls of flour are fried on that fire in whatever grease can be found."[86]

Bridges that link vital parts of towns were favorite target zones for sniper fire. So were intersections, where people left the shelter of buildings to cross the street. One particularly dangerous stretch of road through the center of Sarajevo was dubbed Sniper Alley. Hand-lettered signs on almost every corner warned *Pazi Snajper* (Beware of Snipers). Some ingenious pedestrians learned to take advantage of UN armored vehicles that patrolled the town, walking close beside them and using them as shields against Serb fire.

Serbs kept up the terror by allowing a temporary lull in the shelling, then staging a sudden attack on those desperate or foolish enough to go out. In one such incident in 1994, over sixty-eight unarmed civilians were killed and over two hundred wounded on a Saturday morning when a mortar slammed into Sarajevo's central marketplace.

In another assault in 1992, soldiers in the hills held their fire as a line formed in front of a bakery on Vase Miskin Street. One eyewitness described the horror that followed:

So this morning, a beautiful spring morning, there was an aura almost of tranquillity. And a large number of people plucked up their courage and gathered outside the only bakery still open in our city. People actually crawled out of their shelters and stood in a queue [line]. And then, in a single cluster, the grenades fell on them. Over a hundred people were badly injured and the total of the dead has risen to thirty as I speak. . . . In Miskin Street the blood literally flowed![87]

Soldiers and bystanders carry away the innocent victim of a mortar attack on Sarajevo's downtown marketplace in 1994.

"A Constant Struggle"

Incidents similar to that in Miskin Street have occurred with deadly regularity in Sarajevo, placing an enormous strain on medical personnel who cope with the wounded while also enduring the trauma of starvation, cold, and shelling. Serbs purposefully have targeted hospitals and other health facilities for destruction from the earliest days of the war.

Sarajevo's Jezero Hospital, which once specialized in maternity care, obstetrics, and pediatrics, was hit over 150 times during the first months of the war. Many of its wards, consulting rooms, and laboratories have been reduced to broken concrete shells. Traumatized patients were often rewounded as shells ripped through walls, shattered windows, and

started fires. Temporary wards were set up in the basement for greater protection and to avoid rainwater that sometimes poured through holes in the roof and cascaded down the halls.

In Sarajevo's hospitals, as in hospitals across the country, medical personnel often went without such necessities as X-ray film, laboratory chemicals, and antibiotics while dealing with the most appalling of wounds. Anesthetics were usually in short supply, despite the large numbers of surgical procedures performed daily. Doctors often stanched bleeding and stitched wounds by candlelight when operating room lights were not working.

"It has been a constant struggle being doctors without proper medicines and equipment," said one physician in 1993. "We thought our situation might improve when shelling eased. . . . But then more fighting started . . . and everything just got worse."[88]

Targeting the Young

Along with hospitals, schools were popular targets of assault. By attacking children, Serbs hoped to demoralize and further terrify their enemies. Thus, they timed their attacks for school hours, particularly the recess periods, when children were on the playground.

No children were too young to be spared. "They say shells fell on the Beograd Hotel and on the kindergarten in Dalmatinska Street," reported Zlata Filipovic.[89]

Because of the terrible danger, most schools closed in the first months of the war. "Schools are nonexistent here; the children stay home and cannot go out because the firing is heavier than ever," reported one mother to her daughter who had been sent out of the country.[90]

As time passed, however, teachers courageously organized makeshift schools in their homes or in the homes of interested students. Even at best, conditions were not easy. Male teachers often worked with students during the week, then fought in the front lines on weekends. Students braved sniper bullets to get to class, then later huddled around a stove in the kitchen or worked by candlelight to finish homework. During

These bodies of victims of a Serb mortar attack include a ten-year-old boy killed while playing a game of football.

artillery attacks, studying became even more challenging, as one student wrote to her teacher:

> We have just come up from the cellar because a grenade has fallen very close to the building. When we're in the cellar I study, write, do math exercises and read. . . . I can't wait for this hateful war to end so that I can return to the school I love and see you and all my dear dear friends.[91]

"The Cellar Is Ugly"

Along with artillery fire and sniper bullets, dashes for the cellar were everyday events in wartime Sarajevo. Any activity could be interrupted by Serb attack, and few homes were built strong enough to afford adequate protection for those living inside. High-rise apartments that face the surrounding hills were especially vulnerable. Windows were broken and patched with plastic or cardboard. Walls were pocked by bullet holes.

At night, or when the bombing was at its worst, people gathered in the stairwells of apartment buildings, huddled together on mattresses and blankets and waited for the firing to stop. Others made the hated trip down to the basement. Zlata Filipovic wrote in her diary of one of her first experiences there.

> The cellar is ugly, dark, smelly. Mommy, who's terrified of mice, had two fears to cope with. The three of us were in the same corner as the other day. We listened to the pounding shells, the shooting, the thundering noise overhead. We even heard planes. At one moment I realized that this awful cellar was the only place that could save our lives. Suddenly, it started to look almost warm and nice.[92]

Spies for the Muslims

For anyone forced to endure starvation and cold, dodge bullets, and cower below ground,

---

"Saving Our Skins"

In Sarajevo, cut off from the world for so many months, letters were a treasured means of communication with the outside world. In Letters from Sarajevo, *a compilation of such correspondence, one resident of the besieged city described how she and others cope with the danger all around them.*

"As for us, we are still alive and that is all that matters in this hell. We live one day at a time and are satisfied when the day ends and we are still alive. Every day is the same as the one before, and we no longer notice that they pass one after the other, with no point and no chance of being able to do anything. All we think about is saving our skins, because here life is cheap, it costs no more than a single bullet. And bullets fly about our city like flocks of birds, from one apartment block to another, from one pavement to another. We pass the days in a state of semi-stupor; we hear bombs exploding and wonder what else has been destroyed, and in the evening we congratulate each other—aloud—on the fact that another day is over. Then we congratulate ourselves—silently—for still being alive."

The death rate in Bosnia is so high that parks and other sites have been turned into cemeteries. The above cemetery was once a bustling park in Sarajevo.

staying in touch with the outside world was a top priority for keeping up morale. Serbs recognized this, and concentrated on destroying newspaper offices and television stations as they besieged the capital city.

"The very fine ten-story building that housed the newspaper *Oslobodenje* has been bombed and completely burnt out," reported one Sarajevan to friends in Belgrade in 1992.[93]

Serbs, used to living in a controlled communist society, were also quick to see all journalists as enemy agents whose goals were to carry secret information about Serbs to their enemies, the Muslims. Thus Serb treatment of reporters and photographers was often brutal. Some journalists, such as two newsmen who were captured in 1994, were beaten and interrogated for days before being released. "Every time I would deny that I was a spy for the Muslims and say I worked for [a photo agency], I braced myself for the next blow," said one.[94]

The less fortunate were shot outright as they walked or drove down the streets. By late 1994, forty-six journalists had been killed in Bosnia, more than the number who lost their lives during the entire Vietnam conflict.

Mourners at a funeral are easy targets for Serb snipers. This funeral turned into tragedy when the grandmother of a slain child was herself shot as the family buried the child.

The Rhythm of Death

Soldiers, civilians, the old, and the young regularly fell victim to the shelling and sniper fire that pounded Sarajevo week after week, month after month. "Two, three, ten, fifteen burials a day is the Sarajevan rhythm of passage from life to death," wrote Zlatko Dizdarevic.[95]

In the first two years of the war, ten thousand people, including fifteen hundred children, were killed in the capital city. So numerous were the losses that cemeteries became overcrowded and alternative sites, such as parks and soccer fields, had to be used. Headstones were marked with a simple '92 or '93, to save on dwindling stocks of pre-cut black numbers.

Burying the dead became one of the most dangerous activities Sarajevans could engage in; gathering in open spaces made them easy marks for Serb gunners, who had no respect for their enemies' grief. Burial parties often scrambled for cover behind gravestones when Serbs opened fire in the middle of a service.

In high-danger suburbs such as Dobrinja, trips to a cemetery were out of the question. There, families often used narrow courtyards outside of apartment complexes as temporary grave sites. One Sarajevan described a hasty burial to a friend:

From my window I saw a heartrending scene. My neighbor was killed by a sniper bullet. For several days we tried in vain to take his body to a cemetery. Finally, we had to bury him in front of a building. His friends made a coffin out of a kitchen table and a wooden sign. They managed to bury him, under sniper fire.[96]

Life in a Cage

Despite the desperate conditions under which Sarajevans have existed, ethnic cleansing has not been as successful there as it has been in small villages. Thousands of loyal citizens refused to be driven from their homes. Joked Zlatko Dizdarevic:

There are times when you are ready to pack it in and leave, if only you could, but we've retained something quite essential—a nastiness, out of spite, if you will, or plain stupidity. . . . This is what keeps us here and will probably cost a lot of us our heads.[97]

Others were convinced that their leaving would only play into enemy hands. They rebelled at the thought of Sarajevo's coming under the rule of Serb nationalists. They refused to think that their city could be permanently divided by hate and intolerance. "It will take two generations to heal the wounds in this city, but it cannot be split in two," said Sarajevan Usman Djikic. "Sarajevo was always a city open to everyone. Either we live together or we do not live at all."[98]

"Another Day in Sarajevo"

Children are particularly vulnerable to the nightmare conditions of war, and many have been sent out of the country to be spared the horrors. This poem, published in the book I Dream of Peace, *describes the fear and loss of those not lucky enough to get away.*

"In my dreams, I walk among the ruins
of the old part of town
looking for a bit of stale bread.

My mother and I inhale the fumes of gunpowder.
I imagine it to be the smell of pies, cakes, and kebab.

A shot rings out from a nearby hill.

We hurry.
Though it's only nine o'clock, we might be hurrying
toward a grenade marked 'ours.'

An explosion rings out in the street of dignity.
Many people are wounded—
sisters, brothers, mothers, fathers.

I reach out to touch a trembling, injured hand.
I touch death itself.

Terrified, I realize this is not a dream.
It is just another day in Sarajevo."

Edina, 12, from Sarajevo

Corpses litter a Sarajevo street after heavy Serb shelling. Despite the nightmare conditions in the besieged city, many Sarajevans refused to be driven from their homes and families.

For those who chose to leave, small convoys of trucks were available from time to time. However, the difficulty of getting passports and visas, and the UN practice of closing roads and airports when the fighting was fierce, made travel difficult if not impossible. The most desperate sometimes made a dash for freedom out of the city after darkness fell, but Serb guns with nightscopes made this a deadly gamble.

Whether they have stayed voluntarily or not, Sarajevans have been deeply affected by their confinement. "We live, as it were, in a cage. Every day is the same," wrote one girl.[99] Yet most have retained a stubborn dignity and a perseverance that helps them continue despite the isolation. They are convinced that their city and their culture are worth the suffering.

"Pride is still strong among the 350,000 people of Sarajevo," wrote journalist Roger Cohen, a visitor to the city. "It is rooted in contempt for the marksmen in the hills, for the people who destroy libraries, for all those who want to make a second, 'ethnically pure' Serbian Sarajevo."[100]

Relief agencies and humanitarian groups throughout the world have been touched by the plight of the besieged in Sarajevo and throughout the country. Early in the war, these Good Samaritans stepped in to do what they could to ease the suffering. Their goal has been to bring hope to the people of Bosnia, to let them know that they are not alone.

6 Guardians of Hope

Although the efforts of those who tried to reduce the suffering in Bosnia were not always unified, their philosophy was. It was expressed by Red Cross worker Murray MacDonald, who transported truckloads of humanitarian aid across the beleaguered country.

"I believe that no one should turn their back on aggression," MacDonald explained. "I came simply for that reason. And once I got inside, and saw how desperate it was for people here, I knew it was the right decision." [101]

Red Cross

The International Committee of the Red Cross (ICRC) was one of the first, and largest, relief organizations to enter Bosnia after the war began. The Red Cross's first concern was to investigate whether the Geneva Conventions—internationally accepted standards of treatment for prisoners of war and for the protection of civilians during times of war—were being upheld. In Bosnia, the violations were so widespread and so deliberate that the agency soon abandoned its usual position of neutrality and issued a blanket condemnation. According to one *Time* magazine report:

> After visiting camps run by Serbs, Croats and Muslims, [the Red Cross] found that "innocent civilians" are being held in inhumane conditions by all of them, part of "a policy of forced population trans-

fers carried out on a massive scale and marked by systematic use of brutality," including "harassment, murder, confiscation of property, deportation and the taking of hostages." [102]

The Convoys

Thousands of Bosnians were grateful for Red Cross support and for its protests, which proved effective in improving conditions in many refugee and concentration camps across Bosnia. Relief workers not only inspected camps, they set up and supervised prisoner exchanges between hostile groups and supplied food, medicine, clothes, and blankets to people who were cut off from the outside world.

Canadian truckers Murray MacDonald, John Forbes, and Jerry Avery were three of the hundreds of volunteers worldwide who answered the Red Cross call in 1993. The Canadians were particularly valued for their ability to drive the rugged mountainous roads made treacherous by bomb damage and winter snow. At times, they dodged sniper fire and shells as they drove through embattled areas. "The first shell I heard go off, I was scared out of my mind," admitted John Forbes. "But once you've seen how the people are here—when you go in with your boots and coat and flak jacket and see people standing there in the snow with no shoes—you can keep going, no problem." [103]

Hungry children scramble for food as it is thrown from a UN truck. Food delivery is often difficult; much of the aid never reaches the most needy.

Other Aid

In addition to the Red Cross, the Bosnian people have been aided by a variety of other charitable agencies such as Christian Relief and World Vision, which send food and medical supplies into the country. Doctors, nurses, and other medical experts from organizations such as the International Medical Corps risked their lives working with Bosnian medical personnel to help the injured and traumatized.

Behind the scenes, relief agencies teamed up with corporations so that large volumes of aid could be sent. "Without [pharmaceutical companies'] help, we would most likely not be able to send our current volume of much-needed medicines to people in need," explained Mark Mosley, spokesperson for MAP International, a relief agency based in the United States.[104]

Many of the sick and starving were trapped in besieged towns in eastern Bosnia, however, and received little of the aid. Desperately they waited, hoping that someone would do something before it is too late. "We share every piece of bread, every cigarette," said one woman from Gorazde, who divided her rations—two half-slices of bread—with elderly relatives. "But we're all reaching the point where we can't go on much longer."[105]

In hopes of getting aid directly to the needy, the United States organized air drops of food and medicine beginning in early 1993 and continuing into the following year. Enormous pallets of supplies were transported by plane, then dropped by parachute into target zones in eastern Bosnia. Civilians, afraid that the packages would be intercepted by Serbs, waited eagerly for the drops and scrambled for whatever they could get. Some of the most frantic would-be recipients fought over the packages, stabbing their neighbors in an effort to capture a fair share. Others risked their lives by plunging into icy rivers to retrieve aid that missed the drop point.

Homes for Refugees

Hundreds of thousands of Bosnians not only relied on relief agencies for food and medicine, they counted on those agencies to negotiate their release from refugee camps and to help them find new homes in other countries. The United Nations High Commissioner for Refugees (UNHCR), in charge of finding accommodations, reported large numbers who needed homes, but few countries that offered sanctuary.

"All we get are symbolic gestures from countries who demanded the camps be closed—50 here, 100 there," explained Sylvana Foa, chief spokesperson for the UNHCR in 1992. "Imagine what we would find if we asked for places for two million people. And we have two million people who we consider

A refugee surveys the remains of her home. Relief agencies not only provide supplies to besieged citizens, they also help refugees find new homes.

at serious risk. There is no way we can ask the world to take two million people."[106]

The United States, believing that Bosnian refugees were primarily a European problem, was particularly slow to open its borders. After repeated requests from the United Nations, however, the government agreed to allow 3,000 refugees to enter on the condition that they first obtain sponsors. That lack of sponsorship effectively limited the flow. By May 1993, fewer than 150 had entered the country.

The burden of asylum thus fell on European nations, which were often equally reluctant to take in thousands of people who needed financial support, homes, and jobs. "We all feel like the Kurds," said one former Bosnian truck driver, referring to people who fled persecution in Iraq in 1991. "No place to go and nobody wants us."[107] Nevertheless, over

four hundred thousand refugees eventually resettled in Germany, over sixty thousand each in Austria and Switzerland, fifty thousand in Hungary. Sweden accepted over one hundred thousand before closing the borders in the summer of 1993.

Croatia, at times a political enemy of Bosnia, proved unexpectedly generous in terms of offering refuge to the homeless. Thomas Harrison of the Campaign for Peace and Democracy explained:

> [W]hile extreme Croatian nationalists have demanded a "Greater Croatia" at Bosnia's expense, there has also been broad popular sympathy in Croatia for Bosnian Muslims and the Sarajevo government.[108]

In the first year of the war, over three hundred thousand Bosnians found refuge in

Impossible Mission

Providing aid to war-torn Bosnia is a difficult proposition, one that demands enormous stores of patience and diplomacy. In an article for World Press Review, *French journalist Pierre Hazan describes a Red Cross mission whose purpose was to obtain the freedom of Muslims from a Croat prison.*

"The day for the early release of 500 prisoners has come. A dozen buses flying ICRC [International Committee of the Red Cross] flags have arrived. . . . But once again, everything unravels. Far from the diplomats in Zagreb [Croatia], Perica Pusic, head of the Croat exchange committee and formerly a sales manager in a small store in Mostar [Bosnia], has decided to keep 106 prisoners so that he can exchange them for

Croats imprisoned in Mostar. This is a showdown between law and force, the Geneva Conventions and the Kalashnikov (automatic weapon). After two hours of sordid haggling, he finally brings down his price: All but 53 of the 500 prisoners originally chosen for release can leave. In the courtyard of the detention camp, the [Red Cross] delegates are grappling with a tragic dilemma: Should they 'save' 450 prisoners at the risk of temporarily abandoning the others?

Suddenly, events take a new turn—the Croats revert to their original decision to withhold 106 prisoners. ICRC negotiator Claudio Baranzini refuses to deal. After six hours, . . . failure."

A UN tank rolls by a crowd of citizens waiting to receive aid. While the United Nations continues to provide aid to the battered cities of Bosnia, it has failed in negotiating a lasting peace.

Croatia. Then, because of crowded conditions, the country was forced to close its borders in 1992.

"It's really hard to criticize the Croats," said one aid official. "All their hotels, gymnasia and schools are full of refugees."[109]

A Difficult Decision

Closing the escape route through Croatia added to the desperation of Bosnian Muslims who were running for their lives. Now it was even more difficult for them to leave their country and find asylum.

Some outsiders wondered, however, if the closed borders might be a blessing in disguise. They pointed out that relief organizations are in fact helping the Serbs by moving refugees out of Bosnia. "It would be a wonderful contribution to the Serbian strategy of ethnic cleansing if we did organize the permanent relocation of the Bosnians outside [their country]," pointed out UNHCR executive director Søren Jessen-Petersen in 1992.[110]

That concern seemed irrelevant to some like Patrick Gasser, chief of the Red Cross in Split, Croatia, who had seen thousands of Bosnians suffer and die. "Who is ready to reverse ethnic cleansing at this point?" he asked. "Our question is, 'Who will save lives?'"[111]

The United Nations

It was in an effort to save lives that the United Nations first became involved in the Balkans in 1991, during the war between Serbia and Croatia. In May 1992, fourteen thousand members of the UN Protection Forces (UNPROFOR), known as Blue Helmets because of their bright blue headgear, took up peacekeeping positions between warring parties in Croatia. At that time, Serb–Croat skirmishes continued, but, for the most part, order prevailed.

Bosnians soon discovered that UN efforts were less effective in their own country. In the first months of the war, fifteen cease-fires were signed and immediately broken as Serbs continued to attack towns and villages despite promises to end the fighting. UN sanctions, designed to cut off important supplies of fuel, chemicals, and steel to Serbia, did not stop the attacks. Neither did UN proposals—indignantly protested by Bosnian Muslims—to give almost half of the country to the Serbs if they opted for peace. Serb nationalists protested, too. They had captured more than 70 percent of the country and refused to sign an agreement relinquishing control over any of it.

Completely Neutral

Although UN leaders repeatedly failed at the bargaining table in the first months of the war, Bosnians had hoped for some improvement in their condition as almost twenty-three thousand UN troops entered the country to establish a multinational peacekeeping presence there. Because the UN was concerned that member countries might be drawn into the fighting, however, duties were strictly limited. UN troops were to ensure that humanitarian aid got through to needy civilians. They were not to take sides, nor to participate in the fighting.

Everyone inside the country was quick to see that these orders effectively tied the soldiers' hands. "Our mandate is to protect the UN food convoys and to go wherever they want us. Beyond that we're not in a position to get involved," said Captain Lee Smart, a British member of the UN protection force in 1992. "We are utterly neutral. Should the fighting come past us, under the orders we have been given so far, we can't fight anyone. Should we be attacked, we can defend ourselves."[112]

Despite this limited mandate, UN forces helped save thousands of Bosnian lives. In besieged towns such as Srebrenica and Gorazde, UN aid was all that kept people alive for months at a time. In many cases, however, UN troops were so careful not to exceed their orders that they pacified Serbs rather than stand up to them. When Serbs shot at UN planes as they tried to land, peacekeepers shut down airports instead of fighting. When soldiers stopped and looted UN convoys, peacekeepers explained that their light arms were no match for Serb heavy weapons and rationalized that at least some aid got through.

Bosnian civilians seethed with anger as UN soldiers stood by and did nothing in the face of blatant Serb aggression. The United Nations had designated the cities of Sarajevo, Gorazde, Tuzla, Bihac, Zepa, and Srebrenica as "safe havens" where Muslims were supposedly protected from attack. Yet Serb guns battered those cities to ruin. Helpless civilians were killed and driven from their homes. Serb

Not everyone who comes to help in Bosnia is affiliated with a widely known relief organization. Many people, who often prefer to remain nameless, come for very personal reasons, as Anna Cataldi describes in her book Letters from Sarajevo.

"They were not native to Sarajevo. They came from Jerusalem. They had come to help and they did everything together. They spoke a lot about the work of their organization (the American Joint Distribution Committee) and little about themselves. . . . We later learnt that this 'team' of two had organized the evacuation from Ethiopia, in 1992, of 14,000 Jews in twenty-four hours. . . .

In Sarajevo they were preparing another rescue mission, not only for Jews this time. 'Whoever knocks on this door,' says [one], 'we only ask them two questions: "What do you need?" and "How many are you?" Nothing else.'

. . . . Inside, they served hot soup every day at noon, and then distributed food and medicines. . . . 'Today we're sending out the old, the sick and the crippled. About six hundred of them, people who couldn't survive the winter. . . . We are already in contact with five hundred families in Austria, Germany, the United States and Canada. They will take them in. As Jews we feel a duty to help others, because so many people helped us after the war. And besides, we want to prove to the world that the horrors of the Holocaust will never be repeated.'"

snipers shot down women and children in full view of UN patrols. The soldiers dragged the bodies to safety but did not return fire. Zlatko Dizdarevic reported in 1992:

> In a few months, the Blue Helmets, once the darlings of Sarajevo, have become targets of resentment and scorn. . . . In the beginning, people would approach these boys in the street and shake their hands. . . . Now those feelings have turned, in some cases one hundred eighty degrees.[113]

Danger

The peacekeepers' commitment to neutrality did not protect them from Serb bullets that threatened almost daily. In fact, Serbs con-

stantly harassed and humiliated UN forces, blocked delivery of fuel for convoys, and demanded payment of food and supplies to allow convoys to pass roadblocks. Sometimes the incidents went beyond harassment. In the first two years, seventy-nine UN soldiers were killed; almost a thousand were injured. The UN Security Council condemned the threats and the violence but did nothing to avenge the attacks or to prevent further ones.

"The UN is never going to fight back," predicted one American official in late 1994. "They are intimidated."[114]

In fact, by late 1994, the UN was publicly regretting its decision to put forces on the ground in Bosnia and Croatia. Tension between member nations was high as representatives discussed the wisdom of continued involvement in the region. The effort was extremely expensive, costing over $1.6 billion per year. At the same time, any hint of UN force taken against Serbs carried the very real probability of widespread reprisals against peacekeepers.

For instance, after North Atlantic Treaty Organization (NATO) jets, sponsored by the United States, Canada and Europe, responded to Serb aggression in May 1995, Bosnian Serb forces killed two peacekeepers, then captured nearly four hundred more, daring to use them as human shields by hand-cuffing them to arms depots and bridges that might be attacked by NATO planes.

Even the threat of danger to peacekeepers did not stop the UN from changing its policy in response to Serb atrocities in the summer of 1995, however. At that time, Serb troops overran and brutally cleansed two UN safe havens, the cities of Srebrinica and Zepa, expelling thousands of Muslims, murdering and raping others. Then, in a crowning blow, a Serb mortar slammed into the Sarajevo marketplace, killing thirty-eight civilians and injuring dozens more. Reacting decisively, the UN first pulled the majority of their peacekeepers out of Serb territory. Then, in repeated raids, NATO jets bombed Serb air defenses, missile sites, radar sites, and communication facilities. UN and NATO leaders hoped that such a display of power and resolve would pressure Serbs to consider peace as an option to further destruction.

While many Bosnian Muslims did not believe that the new UN stance would be maintained, others saw the move as a sign of better days ahead. "These were the only detonations of the whole war that made us happy," testified Maida Dajdzic of Sarajevo. "NATO has given us the hope we had lost."[115]

By early 1995, UN leaders were making plans for withdrawing or regrouping their forces, both to widen the options for military intervention and to ensure the safety of UN troops. Ironically, the world's concern for the safety of the troops often distracted attention from the Bosnians themselves, who lived

A UN peacekeeper runs for cover under a hail of bullets. Keeping peace in Bosnia is a dangerous occupation; many UN soldiers have been killed by Serb bullets.

The Peacekeepers' Dilemma

There are no guarantees of safety in Bosnia. Though neutral, UN soldiers often come under attack by Serb troops who see them as enemies. In a New York Times *article, journalist Roger Cohen details an incident that shows the Blue Helmets' dilemma as they struggled to keep the peace in the late spring of 1995.*

"It was a few hours after the NATO air strike. . . . Abruptly, a group of Serbs appeared and fired a volley of bullets in the vicinity of the French [peacekeepers] before demanding their surrender.

'One of my lieutenants called me and said they were under fire and requested my instructions,' [explained their commanding officer Colonel Jean-Paul Michel]. 'As a peacekeeper, it was not easy to know how to respond. I told them to refrain from firing back but not to surrender.'

The Serbs quickly increased the pressure on the French, firing rocket-propelled grenades in their direction. . . .

'I had never faced this kind of decision,' Colonel Michel said. 'We are deployed here as peacekeepers, not as fighting soldiers. I knew I had no way of getting them out and no way of protecting them. I said to myself, "My men are going to die if they start shooting back. And for what? For peace?" So I ordered them to surrender.'"

---

under Serb attack and fought constantly for their lives against tremendous odds.

There is no way to predict exactly what role the UN and other humanitarian agencies will play in Bosnia in the future. Some UN members have long wanted the peacekeepers out of the Balkans, leaving enemy factions to settle their differences on their own. Others believe a continued show of force, such as the NATO bombing raids, will effectively discourage Serb aggression and bring all parties to the peace table.

Agreeing on a new policy has proven almost impossible thus far. However, in the words of U.S. Senate majority leader Robert Dole, "This long-overdue demonstration of resolve [NATO bombing raids] could signal an important shift in the war in Bosnia—if the U.S. and NATO are prepared to stay the course and keep pressure on Serbia and its Bosnian allies."[116]

Holy Warriors

In an effort to help the Bosnians, the mujahedin, fundamentalist Islamic warriors from countries such as Iran, Turkey, and Saudi Arabia, have acted independently of the United Nations and its policies. Several hundred of these men came to Bosnia in the summer of 1992. Their purpose was to train poorly prepared Muslims to successfully fight the war.

"They are very good men," testified Alma Halep, a Muslim girl. "In our country, some of the men don't want to be killed and are afraid to fight. [The mujahedin] are the only ones who have come here to help us."[117]

The arrival of the mujahedin supported Serb claims that Muslims aimed to establish a fundamentalist state in the Balkans. The holy warriors, as the mujahedin were called, had the reputation of being extremists, quick

Few UN troops are more courageous than the Royal Welch Fusiliers, a battalion of almost six hundred soldiers who served with British forces in Bosnia. As journalist Christopher S. Wren reveals in The New York Times, *some of these men were surprisingly young, despite their reputation for toughness.*

"Through a slot in the sandbags, Fusilier [Private] Lee Jones could look down into a green valley where Bosnian Muslims and Serbs were trying to kill one another. He had just turned 18 but he did not announce his birthday for fear that his friends would play a practical joke on him.

The pop of an assault rifle on that day was answered by the rattle of a machine gun somewhere among the fruit orchards and the tile-roofed houses. There was silence, and another exchange of fire. Fusilier Jones lowered his binoculars and picked up a field telephone to report the activity.

'If the war does flame up, it's a good place to observe.' he said."

---

to use force, eager to convert others to their beliefs. They avoided alcohol and believed that Muslim women should wear the chador, a full-length body veil.

Bosnian Muslims had little interest in such practices. Most were moderate in their religious beliefs and posed no threat to non-Muslims. Still, they were grateful for the money and the expertise the holy warriors provided. All were impressed by the bravery of these men, whose war cries to Allah struck terror in Serb soldiers.

"They are very good fighters," said Osman Sekic, a Bosnian woodworker. "They have no fear for their lives."[118]

Despite their expertise, at least seventeen of the holy warriors were killed in 1992 fighting the Serbs. Leader Abu Abdul Aziz was resigned to the likelihood that the death toll would rise. "It will be a long war if the United Nations and the United States don't do anything," he explained. "If the Muslims in Bosnia are not secure, we will fight until they get their freedom."[119]

The Struggle Continues

While people from around the world struggle to bring peace and stability to Bosnia, the victims of the war struggle, too. One year has stretched into two, and then three and still the Serbs continue their assaults. Bosnians now know that peace will not be easy to achieve. The future holds uncertainty and more suffering. As one woman wrote to her children, "All we can do for the present is to try to find the strength to survive until the nightmare is over."[120]

"Maybe We Shall Survive the Horrors . . ."

As long as conflict in Bosnia continues, no one can escape its terrible consequences. The people have tried to make their lives as normal as possible. Still, death and despair have become everyday events. Despite increased world involvement, many Bosnians are unable to believe that the hostilities will ever end.

"I used to have hope, but I can no longer believe we will be saved," said Rosa Tutundzic of Sarajevo. "It will just go on until we are dead."[121]

Coping with Despair

Although continuous physical hardships have been difficult to bear, Bosnians have discovered that the battle against hopelessness and depression was even more formidable. Their country has fallen into the hands of enemies who want to destroy it. World leaders are inclined to appease the aggressors. "We have learned to resign ourselves to everything that's happening. . . . The war has become our routine, our daily bread, our way of life," wrote a teenage girl.[122]

Some have coped with their feelings by making light of the terrible situation. For instance, one teen described how she and her family shared their already cramped quarters with neighbors during the long, dangerous nights of bombing. "We played the hosts on the grand scale, giving them the best places in the cellar. It was a bit of a squash, but, as you know, we stick together."[123]

Some have developed a black sense of humor—finding reasons to laugh at tragic or painful events that might otherwise have made them cry. As one Sarajevan recounted:

There was no electricity—the phones and fax machine were dead, and no radio or television. The only thing that worked this morning was the neighborhood sniper, busy as ever. I would like to know how much they're paying him for all the overtime he's putting in.[124]

Staying Alive

Others find the loss of family, friends, homes, and security nothing to joke about. Suicide and nervous breakdowns have been common. "I am afraid that the bombardment and all these horrors have driven [your aunt] out of her mind," a Bosnian man wrote to his grandchildren. "When I leave home in the morning to go and look for firewood, she kneels in front of the door, and when I get back in the evening I find her in the same position."[125]

Even the most well balanced people sometimes find that the strain of staying alive, of watching others be killed, and of wondering if they will be next sometimes causes them to walk a little slower when they cross a dangerous intersection, just to put an end to the uncertainty.

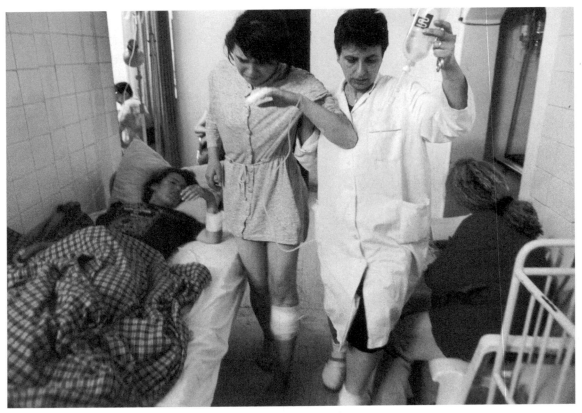

Wounded during a shelling attack, a young girl seeks treatment in an understaffed, ill-equipped hospital. Forced to endure such intolerable conditions, many Bosnians battle feelings of hopelessness and depression.

Anger is another common emotion. Not only are the happy, ordinary days that everyone took for granted blotted out, even the simplest things of life are beyond reach. As Zlata Filipovic lamented:

[I am] a child without games, without friends, without the sun, without birds, without nature, without fruit, without chocolate or sweets, with just a little powdered milk. In short, a child without a childhood. . . . I once heard that childhood is the most wonderful time of your life. And it is. I loved it, and now an ugly war is taking it all away from me.[126]

The most tolerant of citizens cannot contain the hatred they feel toward those who want to kill them and destroy their land. Thousands have experienced atrocities too terrible to be forgotten. Women have been raped. Men have been tortured. Children have been maimed. Zlatko Dizdarevic wrote:

They have taught us to hate. They have made us what we never were—and that is why, though they will be forgiven, we'll find it difficult to do so. It will be difficult for this ravaged Bosnia to return to what it used to be, with the people that we have become.[127]

Scoundrels and Criminals

While most Bosnians grapple with depression, and hatred, others see the war in a different light—as an opportunity to break the law without the fear of getting caught. These criminals, opportunists, and troublemakers have been only too ready to take advantage of the disorder to make money and gain power. Their fellow citizens see this clearly:

Sarajevo is a city of people like any other, heroes and weaklings, cowards and scoundrels great and small, pickpockets and big-time criminals. Some have taken to wartime conditions like ducks to water.[128]

Those who prosper usually do so at the expense of others. Shops that are unprotected by owners are easy to loot. Civilians who are weak from hunger and illness are easy to rob. One man said, "Riso and the Jokic boys chop wood with me and we have to defend it from those cunning rascals who would like to help themselves without working for it."[129] And Zlata Filipovic wrote in 1993:

Electricity is returning to the city. But our crooks, our criminals, our thieves stole the oil from the transformer station, and now almost no one has electricity. Can you imagine? They use the oil in place of gas to drive their cars.[130]

A Little Mood Music

Mark Bartolini, of the International Rescue Committee, visited Sarajevo on Christmas Eve 1994. In a New York Times *article, "Mortars by Candlelight in Sarajevo," he describes the brave attempts at normality that he witnessed while trying to track down a friend in the ruins of the city.*

"After I knocked on one door, a gaunt man opened it and stared at me in surprise. In the background I could see a woman playing the cello by the flickering light of a candle, the sound of shelling and small-arms fire in the background.

When I declined his invitation to come in, he walked away without a word and sat down on the edge of his bed staring blankly out through plastic covering what once had been a window. Books were piled neatly next to an improvised sheet-metal stove, ready for burning when the cold became unbearable. But soon there would be nothing left to burn. (All the available firewood, including the roots of trees, had been cleared from the city.) I kept staring, wondering how they would survive the winter, and then, I left, still looking for the right apartment—the cello music haunting me in the stairwell. . . .

I ate dinner at the heavily damaged Holiday Inn, where the waiters wore tuxedos and white gloves. The decorum seemed appropriate, given that the food, barely enough to be considered an appetizer and anything but a culinary triumph, was nonetheless a logistical marvel.

The mood was further enhanced by candlelight and a pianist, also in a tuxedo, playing 'Moon River.' Accompaniment was sporadically provided by an enthusiastic combo of small-arms fire and mortar-shell blasts."

Black marketeers, people who make a profit from war, are everywhere. Through connections, corruption, and craftiness, dishonest men and women are able to get their hands on luxuries such as cigarettes, candy, and soap, then offer these items for a high price to those willing to pay. Even some UN peacekeepers, in charge of distributing supplies to the needy, have given in to the temptation to make a profit. "They sell ammunition, fuel, and rations. One night, they even got caught siphoning fuel from the tanker trucks that supply Sarajevo," said one French diplomat in 1993.[131] Despite the demand for the items offered, black marketeers are generally despised by honest Bosnians, who believe that putting greed before the sick and starving is an insult to those who do without. Again, Zlata Filipovic wrote:

I went to music school today and saw the marketplace. It's got everything. . . . I wondered where all these things come from and then I remembered my first wartime encounter with the streets of Sarajevo, I remembered the broken display windows and missing goods. Is that the answer? . . . What was done was bad enough, it's even worse to be selling all that now, and to be doing so for expensive foreign money. . . . You should see all the food! Meanwhile we're going hungry and are grateful for anything we can get.[132]

Children of Fear

The war has exposed the dark side of humankind that ordinary children such as Zlata had seldom seen before. Many parents, to spare their children such exposure, sent them out of the country at the beginning of the war. Those who could not get away suffer intensely. Injury, fear, starvation, thirst, and cold are everyday conditions. Periods of shelling and gunfire have been common. In addition, many have witnessed the death of a parent or relative and lived through situations during which they believed they were going to die.

All these events are highly traumatic. For instance, for weeks after eight-year-old Adnan Mujkanovic's older brother was killed in 1994, Adnan was afraid to go outside, afraid even to go to the bathroom alone. "I was left alone once and lost a brother," he

A two-year-old Bosnian stands in a bombed-out section of Sarajevo. He carries a "survival backpack" that his mother made for him in the event of her death. Among its contents are juice and biscuits, the child's passport, and a letter of introduction.

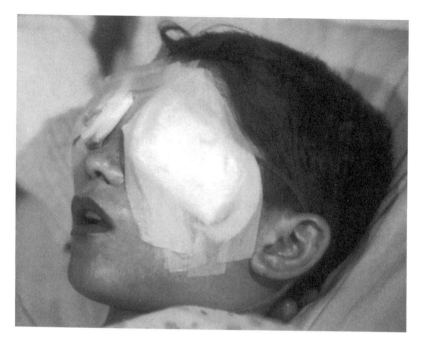

Many children do not escape injury or death. This young Bosnian was severely wounded during the fighting.

explained. "I don't want to be left alone anymore. My brother was my best friend. We slept together in the same bed. We would talk at night about everything. Now it's just me."[133]

Doctors testify that reactions such as Adnan's are not unusual in children who live through war. Many stop speaking, stop playing, and have nightmares. Bedwetting, rebelliousness, and quarrels are common. So is guilt. Many children wonder why they have survived when those they loved have not. Aida Hasimbegovic, a psychologist practicing in Sarajevo, offers this explanation:

> These are normal reactions to an abnormal situation. Children are people without a past. They have had no opportunity to develop coping mechanisms. In many cases, parents here have stopped being good mothers and fathers and children have had to construct their own explanations for this abnormal situation.[134]

Grown Up Too Soon

Some of the most unfortunate children have lost, or have been totally abandoned by, family and friends. With no one to protect them, these children discover just how difficult it is to survive in the midst of war.

"We are without parents, without love, without anything. Our lives are stupid things," said Sanala Beslija, one of over sixty Sarajevan youths who lived in a ruined orphanage in the city in 1993.[135] Sanala and her companions lived in the shadow of fear and violence every day. Not only did they cope with shelling, hunger, thirst, and cold, many had been attacked and raped by their companions and by other street people.

The young vagabonds slept in almost bare rooms and took to the streets every day to find food. On one of these excursions, they met Asif Imamajovic, a thief who took pity on them and shared with them his secrets for staying alive.

"Maybe We Shall Survive the Horrors . . ."

Despite the difficulties of war, the people of Bosnia try to keep their lives as normal as possible. Usually that involves compromise, sacrifice—and danger. Anna Cataldi writes of the difficulties one rather extraordinary girl tried to overcome in Letters from Sarajevo.

"Every morning she jogged around the track circling the grass centre of the stadium now being transformed into a graveyard. She was seventeen, tall, with almond-shaped eyes and hair the colour of dark copper. Silver medal for swimming (I do not remember in which category) at the last Olympics. Since the beginning of the war she had lost two teeth through malnutrition. She asked us if we had any vitamin tablets. She could move faster, she said, than the snipers' bullets. For five months it had been impossible to swim in Sarajevo. Running was essential; without running she would begin to die.

Peter, the German photographer, brought her to the hotel. In the evening she would appear at the journalists' long table and happily eat the insipid fare served up by the Holiday Inn. Peter departed. On the last evening she wore a plum-coloured, almost black lipstick.

We never saw her again, not even on the jogging track."

Imamajovic taught his "students" how to successfully loot stalls in the market, how to elude the police, and how to watch for those who might take advantage of them. "I teach them to steal and not to share," said Imamajovic. "I teach them to survive." Although the children feared their mentor, they were grateful to him as well. "At least he helped," said one. "The other teachers did nothing but wait for the aid shipments, then steal the food and go home."[136]

Post-Traumatic Stress

Children are not the only group to have difficulty coping with the traumatic effects of war. Many adults who have faced periods of acute fear, who have lost their homes, or who have seen their loved ones die often develop serious emotional and physical reactions as well. These reactions, termed post-traumatic stress, are characterized by physical illness as well as deep feelings of guilt, anger, sorrow, or loss. According to the World Health Organization (WHO), as many as one million people in the region suffer from the disorder as a result of war trauma.

One-third of that number are soldiers. Soldiers on both sides of the war are at particular risk of developing post-traumatic stress as a reaction to the ghastly acts they have seen or committed during battle. In early 1995, *New York Times* reporter Stephen Kinzer interviewed a patient in a Croatian hospital who detailed the agony he felt:

My head never stops pounding. I have pain in every bone in my body. I can't sleep, and when I sleep I wake up after an hour because the nightmares are so terrible. I want to stand in front of a mirror and ask why I had to do all the things I did, but I know there would be no answer.

Another man Kinzer spoke to confessed, "[T]he memories don't go away. I was raised as a good Catholic, but now I have no faith in anything. The only thing I believe in now is suicide. I know that very soon I will be in hell."[137]

At a time when the emotional needs of soldiers are judged less important than the needs of displaced and injured civilians, most veterans of the war have not received the treatment they need when they show signs of post-traumatic stress. Yet experts recognize the probability of long-term problems if these men are left untreated. Sufferers are at high risk for alcoholism, drug abuse, suicide, and violence. They can suffer flashbacks, reliving the horrible scenes they have witnessed. They might burst into tears or explode into violence for little or no reason. If untreated, many of these men will have difficulty readjusting to civilian life, holding jobs, and functioning within their families. Their wives, children, friends, and neighbors, already devastated by war, will suffer even more trying to cope with them.

"Based on what we know about Vietnam veterans and Holocaust survivors," pointed out Søren Buus Jensen, a Danish-born mental health professional working for WHO, "there is no doubt in my mind that post-traumatic stress is going to be the most important public health problem in the former Yugoslavia for a generation and beyond."[138]

A Positive Outlook

Despite the terrible effects of war on the citizens of Bosnia, some are able to face the future with a degree of optimism and courage. Young couples fall in love and get married. Adults who have sent children out of the country anticipate future reunions.

Many get through the days by keeping busy. Doctors and other health officials work long hours. So do repair people who restring

Children enjoy a few hours of study in the basement of an apartment in Sarajevo. Despite the difficulties of war, many Bosnians have managed to maintain a positive attitude and look toward the future.

electrical lines, patch gas mains, and lay new water pipes in ravaged areas. Teachers are inspired by their mission of encouraging students who still want to learn. One instructor described wartime schooling:

> We have three classes, three teachers, three blackboards propped up on chairs, all working at the same time. "The only light comes from one small window, but we manage splendidly. . . . The only thing that gives us the strength to go on working is the desire to be of use, to help these poor children to survive.[139]

Perhaps those who feel the greatest sense of purpose are the Sarajevans who defiantly built a secret lifeline, a tunnel, that runs under the city's airport and into a government-controlled suburb on the edge of town. Wounded soldiers who seek aid in Sarajevo's hospitals enter the city through this tunnel. The strongest of the besieged have been able to make their way out into the surrounding hills to bring back supplies and weapons, thus enabling the city to remain free long after it had been expected to fall to the Serbs.

The tunnel was a carefully kept secret for months. It has been heavily guarded by loyal defenders, especially after news of its existence leaked out, to ensure that Serb attacks do not destroy it.

"Nursing Our Mental Health"

Artists and craftspeople are another group of Bosnians who have been noted for their optimism and tirelessness. Many continue to work in make-do studios and theaters, refusing to let the disruption and ugliness of the war defeat them. They put together concerts,

The Tunnel

"What is known about [the Sarajevo tunnel] seems certain to become part of the legend of the war," observed journalist John F. Burns in The New York Times. *As of August 1993, no reporters had passed through the tunnel, and no one had interviewed the builders. Still, some who used the secret lifeline let slip a few details.*

"Like many other improvisations born of necessity in the siege, the tunnel is a Rube Goldberg [make-do] affair, propped up with wooden stanchions and lined with planks. Those who have passed through it say it is excruciatingly cramped, so low that a man must stoop to walk through it and so narrow that only one person can traverse it at a time in either direction.

Since Sarajevo has long been without electricity, the only light in the tunnel comes from flashlights carried by those passing through. Because there is no ventilation, air in the tunnel is sparse and fetid, forcing everybody who enters it to wear a gas mask.

One [Bosnian] who made the trip recently . . . said conditions . . . are so perilous that only people judged strong enough are permitted to attempt it. 'It took me 20 minutes, and I was exhausted,' the man said. 'Once you are in there, you are on your own, no way of communicating, nothing but a flashlight. The air is so dank you think you are going to die.'"

With the threat of death all around, many Bosnians find ways to give their lives meaning. Nino Cengic (holding a fifteenth-century Koran) leads a special brigade to protect the cultural heritage of Sarajevo.

produce plays, and create art shows not only to express their feelings, but to encourage those around them as well. "Work is what makes us hold out," claimed seventy-year-old actress Ines Fancovic. "It's our way of nursing our mental health."[140]

Other artists work to forget their sorrow. "Afan Ramic has had an opening at an art gallery," reported Zlatko Dizdarevic, speaking of a Sarajevo artist in 1993. "His show is an attempt to escape from the fact that he buried his only son, and that the canvases he left at Grbavica [a suburb of Sarajevo] have been burned."[141]

While artists contribute to the positive spirit of their country, they also trade their talents for hard-to-find goods and supplies. In Sarajevo in 1993, one couple designed new I.D. cards for the Bosnian army in return for food—cooking oil, sugar, feta cheese, and peas. After coming up with a new package cover for a Bosnian cigarette company, they were given thirty thousand cigarettes.

Journalist Anna Husarska wrote, "When I mentioned the [U.S.] 'surgeon general's warning,' regarding the dangers of smoking, they joked that in Sarajevo it would be more fitting to print a different warning: *Pazi Snajper*—Beware of Snipers."[142]

Acts of Kindness

In general, people whose convictions and outlook lead them to put others before themselves have coped well during the war. Sometimes the unselfishness is as simple as sharing space in a cellar, offering clothes and blankets to those without, or remembering to bring a child a treat. Zlata Filipovic thought enough of such an event to write about it in her diary: "Zika brought me something wonderful today. A real live orange."[143]

At other times, the gestures demand more sacrifice. Zlatko Dizdarevic recalled a cab driver who had been asked to drive into a dangerous section of Sarajevo:

> Someone told me he hailed a cab last night, after nightfall, and asked the driver—fully expecting a refusal—to take him "as close to Dobrinja as you can." The driver floored it and delivered him to the suburb in record time, reminding him to keep his head down. When they arrived, one of our own on the barricades

Life Goes On

Many Bosnians use the war as an excuse for dishonesty and cruelty. Others, however, discover stores of optimism and unselfishness that they have never called on before. This father's words to his children are taken from Letters from Sarajevo.

"I should like to be able to convince you that there is no need to worry about us or about all those still here who are dear to you. The strength of character people show in adapting to circumstances is quite incredible. I should explain that life here, after the first months of practice in coping with danger, goes on quite normally. People go out, go to work nearly every day, receive humanitarian aid, meet their friends, even go occasionally to a bar despite the fact that there is nothing to drink. . . .

Every war, but especially one like this, forces people to change to some extent. But most of the people who were good and honest will stay that way, even under fire. Unscrupulous people, with no character or morals, will become worse in a war. But, my dears, I want to assure you that when you eventually see those who are dear to you once more, you will not be disappointed."

asked the driver what he was doing in this dangerous neighborhood. And the driver simply said, ". . . This guy isn't joyriding. He must have a reason to come. So I help him." [144]

A Hopeless Cause

Despite the importance of such heroic acts, Bosnia's defenders fear that the cause for which they fight is all but hopeless. Their country has been dealt a near deathblow. There is little likelihood that the struggle can have a happy ending. Still, they hang on for the sake of principle and hope for the best.

As a woman wrote to her grandchild who had been sent out of the country, "Don't worry too much about us. The fate of each one of us is preordained. Maybe we shall survive the horrors and be together again very soon." [145]

A War That Cannot Be Won

The people of Bosnia have been battered by war for over three years. The odds of winning that war have been so slim that the world predicted their surrender long ago. "I think we are on the threshold of the final solution. The main remaining question is the question of maps," boasted Slobodan Milosevic in 1993.[146]

Yet as of 1995, Milosevic's boast had not come true. Bosnia is in shambles, but it is still a nation. The words that journalist Branka Magas wrote in 1992 still apply:

> Despite the cataclysm that has engulfed it, Bosnia-Hercegovina has not surrendered. Its multinational government continues somehow to function. Sarajevo . . . continues to resist. The Bosnian defense forces still contain Muslims, Croats, and Serbs. . . . Bosnia needs outside help, of that there can be no doubt; yet its strength lies in its own determination to survive.[147]

Understandably, war-weary Bosnians are deeply troubled over the future of their country. Given the existing division and hatred, they wonder if the conflict will ever end. They fear the future. As Zlatko Dizdarevic writes:

> Across the ashes of the city, and past ruins we could never have imagined, drift questions that hold sleep at bay just as effectively as detonating mortar shells: What will become of us tomorrow? What will happen to this city, and this country?[148]

Two Possibilities

No one can predict with certainty the fate of the people of Bosnia. World leaders continue to try to engineer a lasting peace; one of the latest attempts was led by U.S. mediator Richard Holbrooke. His 1995 efforts produced another cease-fire, causing the hopeful to believe that a formula for peace may soon be found.

Taking into account the continuing unresolved hostilities, one of two scenarios—or some combination—seems likely to be played out in the future. In the first, Serbs and Bosnian Muslims may be persuaded to sign a UN peace proposal that will result in dividing the country ethnically. There have been many such proposals, and they generally award Serbs almost 50 percent of prewar Bosnia. Thus the country as it was before the war would all but disappear. Remaining Muslims and Croats would have little choice but to relocate into regions set aside for them, or to leave the country altogether. With such a resolution, ethnic resentments would remain, hostilities would be unresolved, and fighting would be almost inevitable in the future.

A second possibility is that the war in Bosnia may continue, even escalate. This scenario reflects acknowledgment that neither side seems willing to lay down its arms. The Bosnian government army, once weak and unprepared, has enlarged its arsenal with captured Serb weapons and with equipment supplied by Iran and other countries. It has

As war drags on, Bosnians continue to cope with a country in shambles.

adopted the successful guerrilla tactics used by Tito's Partisans in World War II and has recaptured some portions of land that had been lost to the Serbs. Its growing confidence is expressed by Bosnian president Alija Izetbegovic. "We shall respond wherever we are attacked and we shall not put up with the shelling and strangulation of Sarajevo."[149]

Meanwhile, the Serbs are just as determined. Some say they are tired of the war, but others seem prepared to fight indefinitely. "I do not mind spending the rest of my life in the trenches if it will finally settle the question of who owns the land," says Nenad Gustimirovic, a Serb soldier.[150]

This balance of strength between sides could cause the conflict to continue far into the future. In the worst case, the war could spread. After several Serb attacks on Zagreb, the capital of Croatia, in 1995, U.S. ambassador Peter Galbraith observed: "Sending a rocket full of cluster bombs into a European capital is . . . an act that can only be intended to provoke a full-scale war."[151]

What Will Be Left?

Whatever the outcome in Bosnia, the war itself cannot be definitively won. Whoever remains will inherit the countless problems of rebuilding a land that is in physical and economic ruin. Homes, businesses, hospitals, and houses of worship are destroyed. Transportation is crippled. Communication systems are cut.

The people are devastated as well. An estimated two hundred thousand have died since fighting began in 1991. Twice that many have been maimed and injured. More than two million people—almost half the prewar population of Bosnia—have been forced out of their homes. Among the dead and missing are leaders whose abilities would have proven invaluable to any restoration effort.

Those who survive are emotionally scarred. Many carry the seed of revenge that could have tragic consequences in the future. "They killed my husband and son," cried one refugee. "They burned our home. But they can never rest easy, because one day we will do the same to them or worse. My children will get their revenge, or their children." [152]

War Criminals

If healing is ever to take place in Bosnia, justice must be dealt out to those who act brutally during the war. As one journalist observed, "No long-lasting reconciliation between enemies . . . can come about without a proper accounting for war crimes; peace is built upon truth." [153]

Amila Omersoftic, a Bosnian Muslim, speaks for millions of Bosnians when she says she will not be satisfied unless that accounting includes the worst offenders—Milosevic, Karadzic, and a few others.

First we have to judge the Bosnian Serb criminals, then perhaps there can be peace. For close to a million unhappy Muslims, I think five Serbs must go to court. That would be reasonable. That would satisfy us. But until then we will just go in circles. [154]

Though reluctant to wage war, the world does not hesitate to acknowledge that Milosevic, Karadzic, and others are morally wrong to pursue their goals of ethnic cleansing. "There is no question about the fact that war crimes have occurred in the former Yugoslavia," states Adam Roberts, professor of international relations at Oxford University. "The Geneva conventions have been obviously and massively violated." [155]

Investigating those crimes and punishing their perpetrators is not the job of one nation. In late 1992, Lawrence Eagleburger, acting U.S. secretary of state, published the

Springtime in the Balkans

In May 1995, Serb rockets fell on Zagreb, Croatia, and Croatian troops pushed back Serbs who had grabbed land in Croatia in 1991. In a Time *magazine article entitled "A Good Season for War," journalist James L. Graff makes the point that a cease-fire does not guarantee peace for the Balkans.*

"When spring comes to the Balkans, so do the rockets, the bullets and the artillery shells. In Croatia the cease-fire brokered by the UN in January 1992 has just suffered its most [outrageous] breach yet. In Bosnia the Muslim-dominated government and the rebel Serbs have both spent the winter arming and training. A four-month-old cease-fire between them expired on May 1. It had begun to break down weeks before, and with the warm weather, the conflict between the parties is sure to intensify.

names of ten men he believed should be tried for war crimes in an international setting. Nazi leaders had faced similar proceedings in Nuremberg, Germany, after World War II.

In support of Eagleburger's actions, the UN Security Council formed a commission of legal experts from around the world to investigate and document allegations of war crimes in Bosnia. By early 1993, three thousand pages of testimony regarding such activities had been sent in by governments, aid organizations, and individuals. Evidence showed that a limited number of atrocities had been carried out by Croats and Muslims. The overwhelming conclusion, however, was that a majority of crimes had been committed by Serb forces under the leadership of Milosevic and Karadzic.

As accusations poured in, the United Nations created an eleven-judge international tribunal to prosecute the crimes. The first trial—that of Dusan Tadic, a Bosnian Serb and former cafe owner—began in May 1995. Tadic was charged with ordering the murder, rape, and torture of Bosnian Muslims in the Omarska prison camp. Other important suspects include the commander of the Bosnian Serb military, General Ratko Mladic, known as the "Butcher of Sarajevo" and Zeljko Meakic, commander of the Omarska camp. Most of the accused remain free in Serb-held territory, perhaps to be tried without being present in court.

"No one knows where this will lead, but we have crimes here of such a scale that you can't just wash your hands of them," stated a Western diplomat.[156]

For Bosnians, promises to bring the criminals to justice are not enough. The powers of the Western world claim to stand for justice and humanity, yet Serb aggression and

We Wait for Peace

After three years of war, there are signs that the fighting in Bosnia may end. The dreams of the children who wait and hope for peace are included in I Dream of Peace.

"War is here, but we await peace. We are in a corner of the world where nobody seems to hear us. But we are not afraid, and we will not give up.

Our fathers earn little, just barely enough to buy five kilos of flour a month. And we have no water, no electricity, no heat. We bear it all, but we cannot bear the hate and the evil. . . .

Our teacher has told us about Anne Frank, and we have read her diary. After fifty years, history is repeating itself right here with this war, with the hate and the killing, and with having to hide to save your life.

We are only twelve years old. We can't influence politics and the war, but we want to live! And we want to stop this madness. Like Anne Frank fifty years ago, we wait for peace. She didn't live to see it. Will we?"

Students from a fifth-grade class in Zenica

A Bosnian soldier mourns over the grave of a fallen comrade in a cemetery that was once a soccer playing field. How many more will perish?

abuse has gone almost unchecked until recently. To Bosnians, that lack of commitment on the part of the rest of the world has been an unforgivable betrayal. Says Mustafa Spahic, a Muslim cleric, said in 1993:

> Bosnia's Muslims are the new Jews of Europe. But we have no America to lean on. We have no one to lean on. . . . This is the first genocide to be committed under the protection of the United Nations. This is the first world-class crime to be carried out like a football game before the eyes of the entire world on television.[157]

Events of 1995—NATO bombing and increased UN involvement—seem to indicate that some of that is going to change. Even if it means standing alone, however, Bosnians are determined to continue fighting for their country and for the ideals they believe in as long as they are able. They have lived through evil days and have suffered disappointment and horror. They have no promise that tomorrow will be better. Still, they continue to endure. In the words of Bosnian prime minister Haris Silajdzic:

> Tanks are hard. Bullets are hard. Bombs are hard. But the spirit is an elusive, defiant power and [the world] did not reckon with it. We were already written off in many quarters, but we are still here ready to fight on.[158]

Notes

Introduction: "As You Can See, Everything Has Changed"

1. Quoted in Roy Gutman, *A Witness to Genocide*. New York: Macmillan, 1993, p. 7.
2. Quoted in Gutman, *A Witness to Genocide*, p. vii.
3. Quoted in Anna Cataldi, *Letters from Sarajevo*. Translated by Avril Bardoni. Rockport, MD: Element Press, 1993, p. 17.
4. Zlata Filipovic, *Zlata's Diary*. Translated by Christian Pribichevich-Zoric. New York: Viking Press, 1994, p. 45.
5. Quoted in Cataldi, *Letters from Sarajevo*, p. 14.
6. Filipovic, *Zlata's Diary*, p. 154.
7. Quoted in Cataldi, *Letters from Sarajevo*, p. 96.

Chapter 1: A History of Division

8. Gutman, *A Witness to Genocide*, p. xviii.
9. Stephen Clissold, ed., *A Short History of Yugoslavia*. London: Cambridge University Press, 1966, p. 61.
10. Quoted in Clissold, *A Short History of Yugoslavia*, p. 63.
11. Quoted in Clissold, *A Short History of Yugoslavia*, p. 111.
12. Quoted in "See Serb Plot in Royal Murders," *The New York Times*, June 30, 1914, p. A2.
13. Clissold, *A Short History of Yugoslavia*, p. 176.
14. Quoted in Lila Perl, *Yugoslavia, Romania, Bulgaria*. Camden, NJ: Thomas Nelson, 1970, p. 69.

15. Quoted in Phyllis Auty, *Tito*. New York: McGraw-Hill, 1970, p. 214.
16. Raymond H. Anderson, "Giant Among Communists Governed Like a Monarch," *The New York Times*, May 5, 1980, p. A1.

Chapter 2: Tito and the Good Life

17. Quoted in Auty, *Tito*, p. 224.
18. Auty, *Tito*, p. 272.
19. Quoted in Auty, *Tito*, p. 274.
20. Anderson, "Giant Among Communists Governed Like a Monarch," p. A12.
21. Priscilla M. Harding, "A Red Cross Nurse in Belgrade," *American History Illustrated*, March 1982, p. 45.
22. Rebecca West, *Black Lamb and Grey Falcon*. New York: Viking Penguin, 1940, p. 23.
23. Quoted in Auty, *Tito*, p. 136.
24. Quoted in Perl, *Yugoslavia, Romania, Bulgaria*, p. 111.
25. Perl, *Yugoslavia, Romania, Bulgaria*, p. 114.
26. Quoted in Perl, *Yugoslavia, Romania, Bulgaria*, p. 127.
27. Quoted in Perl, *Yugoslavia, Romania, Bulgaria*, p. 99.
28. Filipovic, *Zlata's Diary*, p. 11.
29. Quoted in Perl, *Yugoslavia, Romania, Bulgaria*, p. 41.
30. David Binder, "Tito: The Fighter-Survivor Who Unified a Country," *The New York Times*, May 5, 1980, p. A13.
31. "Tito Dies at 87; Last of Wartime Leaders," *The New York Times*, May 5, 1980, p. A1.

Chapter 3: Fury of War

32. Quoted in James L. Graff, "The Butcher of the Balkans," *Time*, June 8, 1992, p. 38.
33. Quoted in Graff, "The Butcher of the Balkans," p. 38.
34. Quoted in Sabrina Petra Ramet, *Balkan Babble*. Boulder, CO: Westview, 1992, p. 165.
35. Quoted in Rabia Ali and Lawrence Lifschultz, eds., *Why Bosnia?* Stony Creek, CT: Pamphleteer's Press, 1993, p. 41.
36. Quoted in Jill Smolowe, "The Human Cost of War," *Time*, November 25, 1991, p. 52.
37. Quoted in James Walsh, "The Flash of War," *Time*, September 30, 1991, p. 39.
38. Quoted in Roger Cohen, "Ex-Guard for Serbs Tells of Grisly 'Cleansing' Camp," *The New York Times*, August 1, 1994, p. A8.
39. Quoted in Cohen, "Ex-Guard for Serbs Tells of Grisly 'Cleansing' Camp," p. A8.
40. Branka Magas, *The Destruction of Yugoslavia*. London: Verso, 1993, p. xiv.
41. Quoted in Gutman, *A Witness to Genocide*, p. xxxii.
42. Quoted in Jill Smolowe, "Land of Slaughter," *Time*, June 8, 1992, p. 32.
43. Quoted in Gutman, *A Witness to Genocide*, p. 81.
44. Quoted in Smolowe, "Land of Slaughter," p. 32.
45. Quoted in Gutman, *A Witness to Genocide*, p. 56.
46. Quoted in Gutman, *A Witness to Genocide*, pp. 36, 42.
47. Quoted in Gutman, *A Witness to Genocide*, p. 37.
48. Quoted in Gutman, *A Witness to Genocide*, p. 55.
49. Quoted in Gutman, *A Witness to Genocide*, p. 47.
50. Quoted in Gutman, *A Witness to Genocide*, p. 68.
51. Quoted in Gutman, *A Witness to Genocide*, p. 76.
52. Quoted in "Land of Demons," ABC News Special, March 18, 1993.
53. Quoted in George J. Church, "Aggression 1, International Law 0," *Time*, July 27, 1992, p. 47.

Chapter 4: Neighbor Against Neighbor

54. Quoted in Ali and Lifschultz, *Why Bosnia?* p. 103.
55. Quoted in Roger Cohen, "Muslim's Ordeal Shows How Ethnic Lines Harden," *The New York Times*, August 30, 1994, p. A8.
56. Quoted in Karen Breslau, "When Marriage Is Sleeping with the Enemy," *Newsweek*, October 5, 1992, p. 52.
57. Quoted in Ali and Lifschultz, *Why Bosnia?* p. xxxiii.
58. Quoted in Breslau, "When Marriage Is Sleeping with the Enemy," p. 53.
59. Quoted in Lara Marlowe, "'Cleansed' Wound," *Time*, September 14, 1992, p. 45.
60. Anna Husarska, "City of Fear," *The New Republic*, September 21, 1992, p. 18.
61. Quoted in Cohen, "Ex-Guard for Serbs Tells of Grisly 'Cleansing' Camp," p. A8.
62. Quoted in Ali and Lifschultz, *Why Bosnia?* p. 111.
63. Quoted in Roger Cohen, "Bosnian Camp Survivors Describe Random Death," *The New York Times*, August 2, 1994, p. A12.

64. Quoted in Edward Barnes, "Behind the Serbian Lines," *Time*, May 17, 1993, p. 34.

65. Quoted in Barnes, "Behind the Serbian Lines," p. 33.

66. Quoted in Marlowe, "'Cleansed' Wound," p. 44.

67. Quoted in Gutman, *A Witness to Genocide*, p. 132.

68. Quoted in Cataldi, *Letters from Sarajevo*, pp. 87–88.

69. Quoted in Chuck Sudetic, "Desperation Drives Escape of Muslim Refugees," *The New York Times*, September 4, 1994, p. A3.

70. Quoted in Michael Montgomery, "Flight of Terror," *Time*, April 12, 1993, p. 38.

71. Quoted in James L. Graff, "The Road of White Death," *Time*, March 15, 1993, p. 45.

72. Zlatko Dizdarevic, "Under the Gun in Sarajevo," *Time*, February 21, 1994, p. 33.

Chapter 5: Sarajevo Under Siege

73. Anna Husarska, "Boom Town," *The New Republic*, August 16, 1993, p. 15.

74. Quoted in Cataldi, *Letters from Sarajevo*, pp. 17–18.

75. Gutman, *A Witness to Genocide*, p. xix.

76. Quoted in Gutman, *A Witness to Genocide*, p. 12.

77. Quoted in Gutman, *A Witness to Genocide*, p. 12.

78. Quoted in Cataldi, *Letters from Sarajevo*, p. 41.

79. Zlatko Dizdarevic, *Sarajevo, A War Journal*. Translated by Anselm Hollo. New York: Fromm International, 1993, p. 40.

80. Filipovic, *Zlata's Diary*, p. 171.

81. Quoted in Cataldi, *Letters from Sarajevo*, p. 45.

82. Quoted in Cataldi, *Letters from Sarajevo*, p. 76.

83. Filipovic, *Zlata's Diary*, p. 69.

84. Quoted in Cataldi, *Letters from Sarajevo*, p. 95.

85. Quoted in Cataldi, *Letters from Sarajevo*, p. 161.

86. Dizdarevic, *Sarajevo, A War Journal*, p. 68.

87. Quoted in Cataldi, *Letters from Sarajevo*, p. 26.

88. Quoted in Dave Manney, "A Bosnian Hospital in a Balkan War," *Medical World News*, June 1993, p. 33.

89. Filipovic, *Zlata's Diary*, p. 143.

90. Quoted in Cataldi, *Letters from Sarajevo*, p. 68.

91. Quoted in Cataldi, *Letters from Sarajevo*, p. 65.

92. Filipovic, *Zlata's Diary*, p. 41.

93. Quoted in Cataldi, *Letters from Sarajevo*, p. 41.

94. Quoted in Roger Cohen, "In Bosnia, the War That Can't Be Seen," *The New York Times*, December 25, 1994, p. E4.

95. Dizdarevic, *Sarajevo, A War Journal*, p. 111.

96. Dizdarevic, *Sarajevo, A War Journal*, p. 22.

97. Dizdarevic, *Sarajevo, A War Journal*, p. 102.

98. Quoted in Roger Cohen, "Under Its Calm, Sarajevo Hides Deep Bitterness," *The New York Times*, January 28, 1995, p. A2.

99. Quoted in Cataldi, *Letters from Sarajevo*, p. 141.

100. Roger Cohen, "Sarajevo, Tired of Being 'a Big Prison Camp,'" *The New York Times*, January 1, 1995, p. A8.

Chapter 6: Guardians of Hope

101. Quoted in Vince Beiser, "Convoys of Hope," *Maclean's*, April 4, 1994, p. 31.
102. Bruce W. Nelan, "Rumor & Reality," *Time*, August 24, 1992, p. 48.
103. Quoted in Beiser, "Convoys of Hope," p. 31.
104. Quoted in Lyn Cryderman, "Some Relief," *Christianity Today*, October 26, 1992, p. 79.
105. Quoted in Graff, "The Road of White Death," p. 45.
106. Quoted in Gutman, *A Witness to Genocide*, p. 104.
107. Quoted in Louise Lief, "Europe's Trails of Tears," *U.S. News & World Report*, July 27, 1992, p. 42.
108. Quoted in Ali and Lifschultz, *Why Bosnia?* p. 184.
109. Quoted in Gutman, *A Witness to Genocide*, p. 103.
110. Quoted in Nader A. Mousavizadeh, "Door Ajar," *The New Republic*, September 21, 1992, p. 29.
111. Quoted in Charles Lane, "Why Are the Camps Still Full?" *Newsweek*, November 9, 1992, p. 37.
112. Quoted in Gutman, *A Witness to Genocide*, pp. 126, 129.
113. Dizdarevic, *Sarajevo, A War Journal*, p. 48.
114. Quoted in Kevin Fedarko, "Bad Blood and Broken Promises," *Time*, December 26, 1994–January 2, 1995, p. 121.
115. Quoted in Kit R. Roane, "For a Change, Crash of Shells Heartens Sarajevo Residents," *The New York Times*, August 31, 1995, p. A1.
116. Quoted in R.W. Apple, Jr., "Airstrikes Armed at Forcing Serbs to Bargaining Table," *Seattle-Post Intelligencer*, August 31, 1995, p. A3.
117. Quoted in Tom Post, "Help from the Holy Warriors," *Newsweek*, October 5, 1992, p. 52.
118. Quoted in Post, "Help from the Holy Warriors," p. 52.
119. Quoted in Post, "Help from the Holy Warriors," p. 53.
120. Quoted in Cataldi, *Letters from Sarajevo*, p. 46.

Chapter 7: "Maybe We Shall Survive the Horrors . . ."

121. Quoted in Edward Barnes, "A City Without Hope," *Time*, July 26, 1993, p. 45.
122. Quoted in Cataldi, *Letters from Sarajevo*, p. 37.
123. Quoted in Cataldi, *Letters from Sarajevo*, p. 19.
124. Dizdarevic, *Sarajevo, A War Journal*, p. 126.
125. Quoted in Cataldi, *Letters from Sarajevo*, p. 123.
126. Filipovic, *Zlata's Diary*, p. 65.
127. Dizdarevic, *Sarajevo, A War Journal*, p. 34.
128. Dizdarevic, *Sarajevo, A War Journal*, pp. 77–78.
129. Quoted in Cataldi, *Letters from Sarajevo*, p. 73.
130. Filipovic, *Zlata's Diary*, p. 177.
131. Quoted in S. Maxime, "Blue Helmets, Black Markets," *World Press Review*, October 1993, p. 17.
132. Filipovic, *Zlata's Diary*, pp. 147–148.
133. Quoted in Chuck Sudetic, "Healing Children, Can Bosnia Heal Itself?" *The New York Times*, June 24, 1994, p. A10.
134. Quoted in Sudetic, "Healing Children, Can Bosnia Heal Itself?" p. A10.
135. Quoted in Barnes, "A City Without Hope," p. 46.

136. Quoted in Barnes, "A City Without Hope," p. 45.
137. Quoted in Stephen Kinzer, "In Croatia, Minds Scarred by War," *The New York Times*, January 9, 1995, p. A4.
138. Quoted in Kinzer, "In Croatia, Minds Scarred by War," p. A4.
139. Quoted in Cataldi, *Letters from Sarajevo*, p. 165.
140. Quoted in Jean Paul Thibaudat, "And Acting Under a Death Sentence," *World Press Review*, April 1994, p. 47.
141. Dizdarevic, *Sarajevo, A War Journal*, p. 171.
142. Husarska, "Boom Town," p. 15.
143. Filipovic, *Zlata's Diary*, p. 184.
144. Dizdarevic, *Sarajevo, A War Journal*, p. 82.
145. Quoted in Cataldi, *Letters from Sarajevo*, p. 166.

Chapter 8: A War That Cannot Be Won

146. Quoted in Jackson, "A Lesson in Shame," p. 38.
147. Quoted in Ali and Lifschultz, *Why Bosnia?* p. 256.
148. Dizdarevic, *Sarajevo, A War Journal*, p. 24.

149. Quoted in Roger Cohen, "As Truce Nears End with No Political Settlement in Sight, Bosnia Rejects an Extension," *The New York Times*, May 1, 1995, p. A6.
150. Quoted in Barnes, "Behind the Serbian Lines," p. 35.
151. Quoted in Roger Cohen, "Rebel Serbs Shell Croatian Capital," *The New York Times*, May 3, 1995, p. A6.
152. Quoted in J. F. O. McAllister, "Atrocity and Outrage," *Time*, August 17, 1992, p. 21.
153. "Making Rules for War," *The Economist*, March 11, 1995, p. 21.
154. Quoted in Cohen, "Under Its Calm, Sarajevo Hides Deep Bitterness," p. A2.
155. Quoted in Bruce W. Nelan, "Crimes Without Punishment," *Time*, January 11, 1993, p. 21.
156. Quoted in Nelan, "Crimes Without Punishment," p. 21.
157. Quoted by Chuck Sudetic, "In Sarajevo, Silence Turns to Despair," *The New York Times*, June 25, 1993, p. A3.
158. Quoted in Cohen, "Under Its Calm, Sarajevo Hides Deep Bitterness," p. A2.

For Further Reading

Anna Cataldi, *Letters from Sarajevo*. Translated by Avril Bardoni. Rockport, MD: Element Press, 1993. A fascinating collection of letters that give firsthand descriptions of life in Sarajevo during the war.

Zlatko Dizdarevic, *Sarajevo, A War Journal*. Edited by Ammiel Alcalay. Translated by Anselm Hollo. New York: Fromm International, 1993. A thought-provoking collection of short newspaper articles, written during the course of the war by a journalist living in Sarajevo.

Zlata Filipovic, *Zlata's Diary*. Translated by Christian Pribichevich-Zoric. New York: Viking Press, 1994. Includes the interests, pastimes, thoughts, and feelings of a young Bosnian girl growing up during the war.

Sonia and Tim Gidal, *My Village in Yugoslavia*. New York:Pantheon Books, 1957. Somewhat dated but interesting account of life in Yugoslavia. Includes black-and-white photos of people, homes, and traditional clothing of the past.

I Dream of Peace. New York: HarperCollins, 1994. A tribute to the children of the former Yugoslavia, with preface by James P. Grant, executive director of UNICEF. A short collection of pictures, poems, and short essays composed by some of those children.

Lila Perl, *Yugoslavia, Romania, Bulgaria*. Camden, NJ: Thomas Nelson, 1970. Interesting details of everyday life in Yugoslavia during the 1960s.

Edward R. Ricciuti, *War in Yugoslavia*. Brookfield, CT: Millbrook Press, 1993. An easy-to-read book that clearly explains the outbreak and early years of war in the former Yugoslavia.

David K. Wright et al., eds., *Yugoslavia*. Milwaukee, WI: Gareth Stevens, 1988. Color photos and text that cover life in Yugoslavia just prior to the war. Includes information about families, holidays, schools, sports, and daily routines.

Works Consulted

Rabia Ali and Lawrence Lifschultz, eds., *Why Bosnia?* Stony Creek, CT: The Pamphleteer's Press, 1993. Fascinating essays that range from the Bogomils to disturbing details of life in present-day concentration camps.

Phyllis Auty, *Tito*. New York: McGraw-Hill, 1970. The complete account of the Yugoslav leader's life, including photos taken during World War II.

Edward Barnes, "Behind the Serbian Lines," *Time*, May 17, 1993. Useful information on Serb soldiers, their attitude toward their Muslim neighbors, and their outlook on the war.

———, "A City Without Hope," *Time*, July 26, 1993. Heartbreaking photos and brief descriptions of Sarajevans and how they cope with the war.

Mark Bartolini, "Mortars by Candlelight in Sarajevo," *The New York Times*, December 24, 1994. A moving account of the author's wartime Christmas Eve in Sarajevo.

Vince Beiser, "Convoys of Hope," *Maclean's*, April 4, 1994. Article on Red Cross truck drivers who risk their lives to deliver relief supplies to starving Bosnians.

John F. Burns, "A Crude 1,000-Yard Tunnel Is Sarajevo's Secret Lifeline," *The New York Times*, August 15, 1993. Fascinating details of the tunnel, and the role it plays in the survival of Sarajevo.

Stephen Clissold, ed., *A Short History of Yugoslavia*. London: Cambridge University Press, 1966. Difficult but complete history of the southern Slavs up to 1966, including hard-to-find details of early Balkan history.

Roger Cohen, "Ex-Guard for Serbs Tells of Grisly 'Cleansing' Camp," *The New York Times*, August 1, 1994. Sobering testimony from survivors of the Susica concentration camp.

———, "Muslim's Ordeal Shows How Ethnic Lines Harden," *The New York Times*, August 30, 1994. Reveals instances of the growing hostility of Bosnian Serbs toward their Muslim neighbors before the war.

———, "A U.N. Commander's Plight: Should Troops Die for Peace?" *The New York Times*, May 30, 1995. Informative article on the danger facing peacekeepers.

———, "Under Its Calm, Sarajevo Hides Deep Bitterness," *The New York Times*, January 28, 1995. Compelling discussion of the need for a just resolution to the war before healing can take place in Bosnia.

Lyn Cryderman, "In the Camps," *Christianity Today*, February 8, 1993. The author spends a day in a refugee camp in Croatia, then travels to Sarajevo and interviews residents there.

Zlatko Dizdarevic, "Under the Gun in Sarajevo," *Time*, February, 21, 1994. The physical and psychological effects of the war on the Bosnian capital as described by a native Sarajevan.

Philip Elmer-Dewitt, "Massacre in the Market," *Time*, February 14, 1994. An account of one of the bloodiest air attacks in the war.

James L. Graff, "The Butcher of the Balkans," *Time*, June 8, 1992. Informative article on the background and philosophy of Slobodan Milosevic, president of Serbia.

———, "A Good Season for War," *Time*, May 15, 1995. An account of Serb attacks on Zagreb, the capital of Croatia, in 1995.

———, "Murder at Ugar Gorge," *Time*, October 12, 1992. Graphic account of mass murder in Bosnia as told to a *Time* reporter by a survivor.

———, "The Road of White Death," *Time*, March 15, 1993. A brief but moving article on the survival efforts of the besieged residents of Gorazde.

Roy Gutman, *A Witness to Genocide*. New York: Macmillan, 1993. Includes information about the first days of the war, as well as very disturbing accounts of atrocities carried out by Serbs in 1992–93.

Pierre Hazan, "With the Red Cross in Bosnia," *World Press Review*, January 1994. The difficulties the Red Cross faces as it goes about its work in the war.

Anna Husarska, "Boom Town," *The New Republic*, August 16, 1993. Fascinating examples of the indomitable spirit that helps Bosnian artists survive.

———, "City of Fear," *The New Republic*, September 21, 1992. Useful details of life in the Serb-dominated Bosnian cities of Banja Luka and Celinac.

Stephen Kinzer, "In Croatia, Minds Scarred by War," *The New York Times*, January 9, 1995. Informative article on the long-term psychological effects of war on soldiers in Bosnia.

Charles Lane, "Why Are the Camps Still Full?" *Newsweek*, November 9, 1992. The problem of finding asylum for refugees, plus a discussion of whether humanitarian efforts are aiding ethnic cleansing.

Sidney Lens, "The Promise of Self-Management," *The Progressive*, October 1981. Easy-to-read article on socialism in Yugoslavia in the early 1980s.

Louise Lief, "Europe's Trail of Tears," *U.S. News & World Report*, July 27, 1992. An alarming comparison of the Holocaust and ethnic cleansing in Bosnia.

Dave Manney, "A Bosnian Hospital in a Balkan War," *Medical World News*, June 1993. Informative piece detailing the extreme difficulties health workers face in Bosnia.

Lara Marlowe, "'Cleansed' Wound," *Time*, September 14, 1992. Unique look at ethnic cleansing from a Serb point of view.

Michael Montgomery, "Flight of Terror," *Time*, April 12, 1993. Short report and photos of Muslim refugees who stampeded for places on a UN relief convoy with disastrous effect.

Nader A. Mousavizadeh, "Door Ajar," *The New Republic*, September 21, 1992. A thought-provoking discussion of the Bosnian refugee problem.

The New York Times, "Heir to Austria's Throne Is Slain with His Wife by a Bosnian Youth to Avenge Seizure of His Country," June 29, 1914. Lengthy article written at the time of the infamous assassination.

Tom Post, "Help from the Holy Warriors," *Newsweek*, October 5, 1992. An easy-to-read account of the mujahedin warriors who have trained Bosnia's Muslims to fight.

Jill Smolowe, "Land of Slaughter," *Time*, June 8, 1992. Sobering facts and photos that detail the first weeks of the war.

Thomas H. Stahel, "A U.S. Archbishop Visits Croatia and Bosnia," *America*, September 12, 1992. An interview that includes a firsthand account of panicky refugees fleeing from Serb aggression.

Chuck Sudetic, "Healing Children, Can Bosnia Heal Itself?" *The New York Times*, June 24, 1994. Informative discussion of the psychological damage the war has produced in Bosnian children.

Jean Paul Thibaudat, "And Acting Under a Death Sentence," *World Press Review*, April 1994. Uplifting picture of the artistic community in Sarajevo and its invaluable contribution to the war effort.

Rebecca West, *Black Lamb and Grey Falcon*, 1940. Reprint, New York: Penguin Books, 1982. A thousand-page volume that describes the author's journey through Yugoslavia prior to World War II. Includes colorful details regarding the people and history of the region.

Naida Zecevic, "Will I Ever Go Home Again?" *Newsweek*, March 8, 1993. Reflections on the Bosnian war by an eighteen-year-old Sarajevan who fled the country early in the conflict.

Index

Picture Credits

Cover photo by The Bettmann Archive
AP/Wide World Photos, 9, 11, 25, 42, 44, 46, 61, 62, 64, 67, 70, 73, 78, 84, 85, 87, 92, 95
The Bettmann Archive, 16
Alexander Boulat/Sipa Press, 60
National Archives, 18

Reuters/Bettmann, 8, 34, 37, 39, 40, 48, 51, 52, 54, 65, 68, 72, 75, 82
Sipa Press, 26, 28, 30
Stock Montage, 15
UPI/Bettmann, 17, 19, 23, 57
Teun Voeten/Impact Visuals, 43, 59, 89

About the Author

Diane Yancey began writing for her own entertainment when she was thirteen, living in Grass Valley, California. Later she graduated from Augustana College in Illinois. She now pursues a writing career in the Pacific Northwest, where she lives with her husband, two daughters, and two cats. Her interests include collecting old books, building miniature houses, and traveling.

Ms. Yancey's books include *Desperadoes and Dynamite*, *The Reunification of Germany*, *The Hunt for Hidden Killers*, *Zoos*, *Schools*, and *Camels for Uncle Sam*.

j949.742   Yancey, Diane.
YAN
          Life in war-torn
          Bosnia.

$22.59   FEB 12 1996

DATE